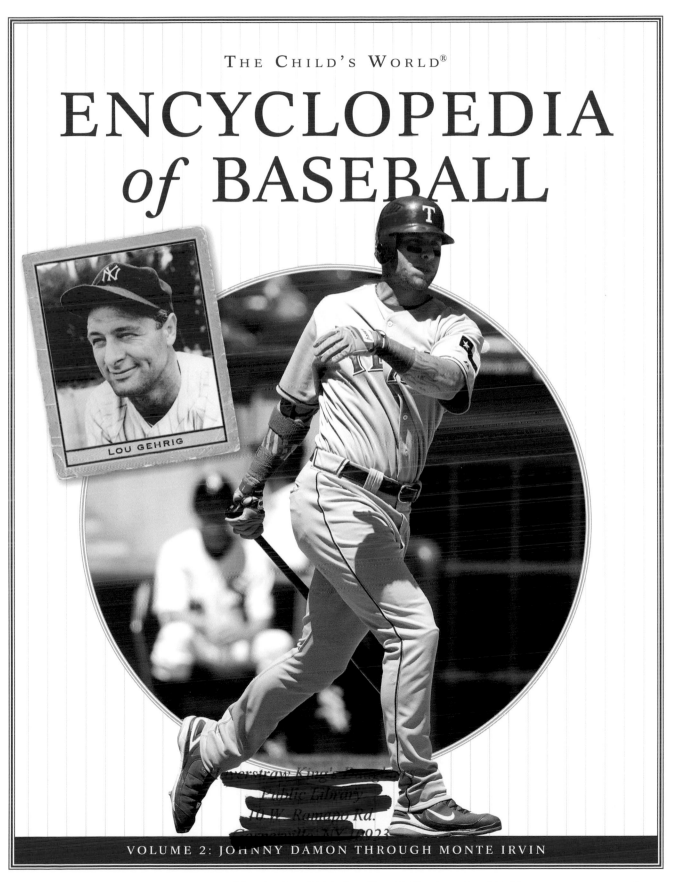

THE CHILD'S WORLD®

ENCYCLOPEDIA
of BASEBALL

LOU GEHRIG

VOLUME 2: JOHNNY DAMON THROUGH MONTE IRVIN

By James Buckley, Jr., David Fischer, Jim Gigliotti, and Ted Keith

KEY TO SYMBOLS

Throughout *The Child's World® Encyclopedia of Baseball*, you'll see these symbols. They'll give you a quick clue pointing to each entry's general subject area.

Active player   **Baseball word or phrase**   **Hall of Fame**   **Miscellaneous**   **Ballpark**   **Team**

The Child's World
www.childsworld.com

Published in the United States of America by The Child's World®
1980 Lookout Drive, Mankato, MN 56003-1705
800-599-READ • www.childsworld.com

ACKNOWLEDGMENTS

The Child's World®: Mary Berendes, Publishing Director

Produced by Shoreline Publishing Group LLC
President / Editorial Director: James Buckley, Jr.
Cover Design: Kathleen Petelinsek, The Design Lab
Interior Design: Tom Carling, carlingdesign.com
Assistant Editors: Jim Gigliotti, Zach Spear

Cover Photo Credits: Focus on Baseball (main); National Baseball Hall of Fame Library (inset).
Interior Photo Credits: AP/Wide World: 8, 12, 13, 15, 19, 20, 21, 23, 28, 30, 31, 32, 35, 36, 41, 42, 43, 45, 48, 49, 50, 52, 53, 56, 57, 59, 61, 63, 64, 65, 67, 70, 72, 75, 76, 81, 83; Corbis: 10, 26, 27, 40, 46, 47, 80; Focus on Baseball: 4, 5, 6, 9, 11, 16, 18, 24, 25, 33, 37, 39, 44, 54, 58, 62, 65, 66, 69, 71, 73, 74, 78, 79; Getty Images: 60; iStock: 51, 68; Al Messerschmidt: 22, 29, 34, 38, 64, 77; National Baseball Hall of Fame Library: 14.

LIBRARY OF CONGRESS CATALOG-IN-PUBLICATION DATA

The Child's World encyclopedia of baseball / by James Buckley, Jr. ... [et al.].
    p. cm. – (The Child's World encyclopedia of baseball)
  Includes index.
  ISBN 978-1-60253-167-3 (library bound : alk. paper)–ISBN 978-1-60253-168-0 (library bound : alk. paper)–ISBN 978-1-60253-169-7 (library bound : alk. paper)–ISBN 978-1-60253-170-3 (library bound : alk. paper)–ISBN 978-1-60253-171-0 (library bound : alk. paper)
  1. Baseball–United States–Encyclopedias, Juvenile. I. Buckley, James, 1963- II. Child's World (Firm) III. Title. IV. Series.

GV867.5.C46 2009
796.3570973–dc22

2008039461

■ *The great catcher Josh Gibson.*

PEOPLE HAVE BEEN PLAYING BASEBALL, America's national, pastime, for more than 150 years, so we needed a lot of room to do it justice! The five big volumes of *The Child's World Encyclopedia of Baseball* hold as much as we could squeeze in about this favorite sport.

The Babe. The Say-Hey Kid. The Iron Horse. The Splendid Splinter. Rapid Robert. Hammerin' Hank. You'll read all about these great players of yesterday. You'll also learn about your favorite stars of today: Pujols, Jeter, Griffey, Soriano, Santana, Manny, and Big Papi. How about revisiting some of baseball's most memorable plays and games?

The Shot Heard 'Round the World. The Catch. The Grand-Slam Single. You'll find all of these—and more.

Have a favorite big-league team? They're all here, with a complete history for each team that includes its all-time record.

Ever wonder what it means to catch a can of corn, hit a dinger, or use a fungo? Full coverage of baseball's unique and colorful terms will let you understand and speak the language as if you were born to it.

This homegrown sport is a part of every child's world, and our brand-new encyclopedia makes reading about it almost as fun as playing it!

■ *Florida's World Series trophy.*

Contents: Volume 2: Johnny Damon >> Monte Irvin

■ *Damon moved to New York after starring in Boston.*

Damon will forever be remembered for his huge role with the 2004 Boston Red Sox, the team that broke the "Curse of the Bambino." The Sox dropped the first three games of the 2004 American League Championship Series to New York, and no team had ever come back from such a deficit. The Sox won the following three games and forced a deciding seventh game in Yankee Stadium. Damon had the greatest game of his career to complete the amazing comeback. He singled in the first inning, hit a grand slam home run in the second inning, and then hit a two-run homer in the fourth inning to lead the Sox into the World Series. Boston then swept the St. Louis Cardinals to win the championship, their first since 1918.

Boston fans adored Damon's gritty play, as well as his flowing long hair and shaggy beard. He even earned the nickname "Captain Caveman" in honor of his fuzzy appearance.

Damon, Johnny

Johnny Damon has been one of the most popular and fan-friendly players since his career began with the Kansas City Royals in 1995. The left-handed hitting center fielder has more than 2,000 hits and 300 stolen bases for the Royals, A's, Red Sox, and Yankees.

Following an All Star season in 2005 with Boston, Damon signed a free-agent contract with the New York Yankees. Red Sox Nation felt betrayed. As a Yankee, Damon keeps his hair short and is clean-shaven, but his ability to hit in the clutch remains. In eight postseason games with New York, he has hit three homers and driven in eight runs.

Dandridge, Ray

Ray Dandridge was one of the greatest defensive third basemen ever, and he is generally regarded as the greatest third baseman in Negro League history. He played mostly with the Newark Eagles in the 1930s. He went to play in the Mexican League in 1940, and excelled there and in Cuba, while continuing to be shut out of the segregated Major Leagues. Although the Major Leagues integrated in 1947, it was too late for Dandridge. He was still a productive hitter, but he was in his mid-30s by that time. In 1951, while playing for Minneapolis, a minor-league team affiliated with the National League's New York Giants, he mentored a young outfielder named Willie Mays, who was called up to the big leagues later that year.

Dandridge was selected to the Hall of Fame by the Veteran's Committee in 1987. He followed nine other Negro Leaguers into the Hall.

Dead-ball Era

This was the nickname of the period from 1900 to 1919 when the baseball was soft and loosely wound. Therefore, it didn't travel far when hit. During those years, players such as Frank "Home Run" Baker led the league with just 10 or 12 homers in a season. The game was dominated by great pitchers such as Cy Young, Walter Johnson, and Christy Mathewson.

Baseball's rules changed in 1920, however, making the ball more tightly wound and livelier when batters hit it. And if a ball was dirty, umpires replaced it with a clean ball. After the rules changes, batters during the 1920s could see the ball better and hit the ball farther than ever before.

Dean, Dizzy

Jay Hannah "Dizzy" Dean, a right-handed pitcher for the St. Louis Cardinals, was one of the best and most colorful pitchers of all time. In 1934, he had one of the greatest single seasons a pitcher has ever had. He won 30 games for St. Louis' "Gashouse Gang" and had an earned run average of 2.66 (when the league average was over 4.00). Dizzy was the MVP of the National League that season. Dean also won two games in the World Series in 1934. The other two Cardinals' victories in that World Series were supplied by Dizzy's brother, Paul "Daffy" Dean.

In Game Four of that '34 World Series, Dizzy was sent in the game as a pinch-runner. The next batter hit a ground ball, and Dean broke up the potential double-play by throwing his body in front of the thrown ball. The ball struck him in the head, knocking him out and sending him to the hospital. (Headlines the next day were memorable, and poked fun at Dizzy's lack of education: "X-rays of Dean's head reveal nothing.") Dizzy recovered to pitch (and win) the fifth and seventh games of that World Series.

Far from a one-year wonder, Dizzy was second in the N.L. MVP voting in 1935 with a 28–12 record and in 1936 with a 24–13 mark. However, Dizzy's career was never the same following an injury suffered in the 1937 All-Star Game. His toe was broken by a line drive. Dean altered his pitching motion to help heal the broken toe, and he injured his throwing arm in the process. He was traded to the Chicago Cubs in 1938 at the age of 28, but won

■ *The Federal League lasted only two years.*

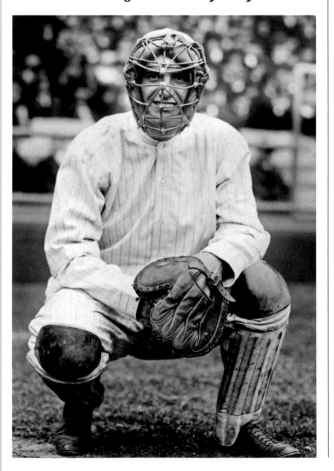

only 16 games the remainder of his career. He overall career record was 150–83. The four-time 20-game winner was elected to baseball's Hall of Fame in 1953.

Known for his misuse of grammar– "The runner slud into third"–Dean was one of the first and most popular baseball commentators, working for ABC and CBS throughout the 1950s. He died in 1974, at the age of 64.

Defunct Leagues

In 1858, 12 years after the Knickerbocker Base Ball Club of New York played its first game at the Elysian Fields, the Knickerbockers and 20 other teams from the New York City area formed the National Association of Base Ball Players (NABBP). According to association rules, all players had to be amateurs. By 1865, the league had grown to 60 teams. But as more teams were formed, the demand for good players grew, and some teams began paying top players under the table.

In 1869, Harry Wright, the player-manager of the Cincinnati Red Stockings, decided to openly offer salaries to the best players he could find. He signed nine players to average annual contracts of $950, and the first baseball team composed completely of professionals was formed. The Red Stockings (who still play in Cincinnati but are now known simply as the Reds) soon had other openly pro teams to play.

In 1871, Wright and nine of his associates broke away from the National Association of Base Ball Players, which still claimed to be for amateurs only, and formed a new organization called the National Association of Professional Base Ball Players. This was the first major pro league. The league collapsed after five seasons, in 1875. The next year, the National League played its first game and has not looked back since.

Other leagues trying to compete with the dominant National League came and went between 1877 and 1892. The American Association, formed in 1882, was the most successful, perhaps because team owners played games on Sundays and sold beer. The "Beer and Whiskey League," as it was known, lasted 10 seasons but folded after the 1891 season.

Ten years later, in 1901, the American League began playing under the accepted National League rules. The American League was soon considered equal to the National League. Baseball was becoming a profitable business. In 1914, a third league, calling itself the Federal League, declared itself a major league, and began buying star ballplayers from the National and American Leagues.

The upstart Federal League, bogged down by lawsuits from the other two leagues, had trouble meeting its financial obligations in 1915. After the season, the

■ *Delgado has been a slugger for three teams.*

Federal League folded. No rival baseball league has since competed against the American and National Leagues.

For a list of long-ago pro baseball leagues, see the Appendix, page 84.

Delgado, Carlos

Carlos Delgado has been one of baseball's best power hitters of the early 2000s. He began his career in 1994 with the Toronto Blue Jays. The first baseman

continued on page 10

■ *Hank Greenberg, a Tigers all-time hero.*

Detroit Tigers

The Detroit Tigers were one of the first teams of the American League, beginning in 1901. The Tigers first great player was outfielder Sam "Wahoo" Crawford, who jumped to the club from the National League's Reds in 1902. The best player in franchise history—maybe the best in baseball history—was Ty Cobb, who joined the Tigers in August, 1905. Cobb batted .367 over his 24-year career, and his 4,191 hits were the most for decades until Pete Rose surpassed the mark in the 1980s.

Cobb and Crawford led the Tigers to the 1907 pennant, but the team came up short in the World Series against the Cubs. The Tigers repeated their A.L. pennant in 1908. Once again, they lost to the Cubs in the World Series. In 1909, the Tigers went to the World Series for the third straight year, but lost to the Pittsburgh Pirates.

The Tigers enjoyed little success in the 1920s. In the 1930s, second baseman Charlie Gehringer and first baseman Hank Greenberg began their great careers. Despite winning the A.L. pennant in 1934, the Tigers fell to St. Louis' "Gashouse Gang" in the deciding seventh game.

In 1935, the Tigers finally won the World Series, despite an injury to superstar Greenberg in the second game. Greenberg also lost more than four prime years of his career to military service, but he returned in mid-season 1945, in time to decide the pennant race with a grand slam on the final day of the season. The Tigers defeated the Cubs in seven games for another World Series title.

Despite some good players such as third baseman George Kell and right fielder Al Kaline, the Tigers slipped into the second division of the American League during the 1950s. Following their 1945 title, the Tigers finished at least 10 games behind the pennant winner 19 of 21 seasons.

The Tigers righted themselves in the late 1960s, but lost the 1967 pennant on the final day of the season to the Red Sox. The next year, the Tigers brought the racially divided city of Detroit together by winning 103 games and coasting to the pennant. Denny McLain won 31 games to capture both the MVP and Cy Young Award. No pitcher has won 30 games in a season since McLain, but it was another hurler, Mickey Lolich, who stole the show in October. Lolich won three games in the 1967 World Series—outdueling the Cardinals' ace Bob Gibson in the seventh game—to give Detroit the Series victory.

In 1976, Detroit pitcher Mark "The Bird" Fidrych surprised everyone and became a national hero, if only for a little while. He talked to the baseball, got down on his hands and knees to landscape the mound, and he mowed down opposing hitters. He won 19 games and led the league in earned run average. But Fidrych's stardom was short-lived, as he was hurt the following year and only won a handful more games before retiring after a short career.

In 1984, under manager Sparky Anderson, the Tigers began the season by winning 35 of their first 40 games, and finished in first place by 15 games. Detroit fans listened to revered announcer

Ernie Harwell describe their team's sweep of the Royals in the A.L. playoffs, and then defeat the Padres in five games in the World Series. One key reason was the steady play of shortstop Alan Trammell, the Series Most Valuable Player.

Trammell played for the Tigers for 20 seasons, beginning in 1977. The Tigers turned to him to manage the team in 2003. It was a miserable season, with the young and inexperienced Tigers losing 119 games, an American League record for defeats. Two seasons later, Trammell was replaced by Jim Leyland, who had managed the 1997 Marlins to the World Series title. Leyland took over a 71-win team and, by the very next season, the Tigers were 95–67 and in the postseason. They defeated the New York Yankees and Oakland A's to return to the World Series, where they fell to the St. Louis Cardinals in five games.

■ *Tigers slugger Magglio Ordoñez.*

DETROIT TIGERS

LEAGUE: **AMERICAN**

DIVISION: **EAST**

YEAR FOUNDED: **1901**

CURRENT COLORS:
BLACK AND ORANGE

STADIUM (CAPACITY):
**COMERICA PARK
(40,950)**

ALL-TIME RECORD
(THROUGH 2008):
8,478–8,279

WORLD SERIES TITLES
(MOST RECENT):
4 (1984)

has also played for the Florida Marlins (2005), and New York Mets (beginning in 2006). In a 10-year stretch beginning in 1997, Delgado hit 370 home runs. Despite his 431 career home runs through the 2007 season, he has never finished first or second in homers in his league.

Delgado is one of 15 Major Leaguers to hit four home runs in one game. He accomplished the feat on September 25, 2003 for the Blue Jays against the Devil Rays.

A native of Puerto Rico, Delgado is perhaps second only to Roberto Clemente as the best player to come from that island. Delgado is also politically-minded like his idol. In 2004, Delgado stayed in the dugout during the seventh-inning stretch when "God Bless America" was played, to respectfully protest U.S. involvement in Iraq.

Designated Hitter

A player put in a permanent spot in the batting order to replace the pitcher. In 1973, the American League adopted the designated hitter rule in the hopes of increasing scoring and boosting attendance. Most pitchers are poor hitters, and the rule change gave A.L. teams an additional bat in the lineup. This was baseball's biggest rule change of the century. The National League refused to adopt the designated hitter rule, and the two leagues have played under different rules ever since. (Players other than the pitcher can be replaced by a DH, but this is almost never done.)

In 1973, Ron Blomberg of the New York Yankees became the first player ever to bat as a designated hitter. He drew a bases-loaded walk against the Red Sox in the first inning on Opening Day in 1973 at Boston's Fenway Park.

Detroit Tigers

Please see pages 8–9.

■ *Slugger Frank Thomas was a top designated hitter.*

■ *This photo of Cincinnati's Great American Ballpark shows the "diamond" formed by the four bases.*

Diamond

Another word for the baseball infield, due to the shape the four bases form. Though it refers just to the infield, the word is also used to describe an entire baseball field.

Dickey, Bill

Bill Dickey was one of the greatest catchers in baseball history. Credited by some for calling the catchers' gear "the tools of ignorance," he played for the New York Yankees between 1928 and 1946. Dickey also managed the Yankees in 1946, and was a coach with the team throughout the 1950s. He played with Babe Ruth, Lou Gehrig, and Joe DiMaggio, and he mentored a young Yogi Berra.

Dickey was known as a great handler of pitchers, and played a key role on dominant title teams. He was also one of the finest-hitting catchers of all time. He batted .300 in 10 different seasons, including

continued on page 14

DiMaggio, Joe

Joe DiMaggio is one of the best-remembered and greatest ballplayers ever. A right-handed hitting outfielder, he played for the New York Yankees from 1936-1951. He was a majestic center fielder, known for his grace and elegance.

DiMaggio followed his older brother Vince to the San Francisco Seals of the Pacific Coast League (a notch below the Major League level) in 1933. As an 18-year old, Joe hit in 61 consecutive games for the Seals. By 1936, he was in the Major Leagues with the New York Yankees, playing alongside the great Lou Gehrig. DiMaggio was a big hit with fans in New York City, which had a large Italian immigrant population. In his rookie year, he hit 29 home runs, 15 triples, 44 doubles, and drove in 125 runs—despite missing 16 games with an injury.

In 1937, he was even better. He hit 46 home runs (and struck out a mere 37 times) while driving in 167 runs and scoring 151.

DiMaggio had a great eye, as the numbers suggest: In his 13-year career, he struck out only 367 times.

The Yankees won the World Series in DiMaggio's first four seasons with the club (1936–39). In all, he played on nine World Series-winning teams.

The "Yankee Clipper" won batting titles in 1939, at .381, and 1940, at .352. (He got his nickname from a type of fast-sailing ship. Many said he resembled a smooth sailer as he moved through the outfield.). In 1941, he accomplished something that has stood the test of time.

■ *Few players have been as well-loved as DiMaggio.*

He got at least one hit in 56 consecutive games. In those 56 games, he reached base 112 times (91 hits, 21 walks). He struck out just seven times. After being held hitless in a 57th game by the Cleveland Indians (third baseman Ken Keltner famously made two great plays to rob him of hits), DiMaggio hit safely in his next 16 games, for an astonishing total of hitting safely in 72 of 73 games. No player since has come closer than 44 straight games with a hit. DiMaggio won the MVP that year (his third award), beating Ted Williams in a season in which Williams batted over .400.

In DiMaggio's first six seasons, he averaged .345 and 33 home runs a season. But he lost time in the prime of his career (as did many of his fellow players), when he entered the service with his country at war. DiMaggio didn't play in 1943, 1944, or 1945, spending time instead in the U.S. Army, though he often played on Army All-Star teams or visited with fellow soldiers as a sports celebrity. He did not participate in armed combat. After the war ended, DiMaggio returned to the Yankees in 1946.

However, the Clipper never sailed quite as well after the war. In 1947, a bone spur was taken from Joe's left heel. Before the 1948 season, doctors removed bone chips from his throwing elbow. After that season, he had problems with his right heel that

■ *DiMaggio often appeared at baseball events.*

kept him from playing the first half of the 1949 season. Finally, frustrated with battling injuries, he retired in 1951 at the age of 36, rather than play with diminishing skills.

After retirement, DiMaggio was briefly married to Hollywood actress Marilyn Monroe. Throughout the 1960s and 1970s, he often appeared at Yankee Stadium and did work in TV commercials. He was named "The Greatest Living Player" in 1969, and held the title for 30 years, until his death in 1999 at the age of 84.

a career high .362 average in 1936. He was the A.L.'s starting catcher in six of the first eight All-Star Games.

Dickey's Yankees won seven World Series. He caught at least 100 games for 13 consecutive seasons, a record that wasn't equaled until Johnny Bench accomplished it in the 1970s. Dickey earned 17 World Series rings as a player or coach—more than anyone in history not named Yogi Berra.

Dickey was inducted into the Baseball Hall of Fame in 1954.

■ *Cuba's Martin Dihigo could do it all on a baseball field.*

Dihigo, Martin

Martin Dihigo was a great Cuban ballplayer who played mostly in the 1920s and '30s. He is a member of Halls of Fame in four different countries: the United States, Cuba, Mexico, and Venezuela.

Dihigo had the ability to play all nine positions well, including pitcher. Dihigo began his career in the United States in 1923 as a first and second baseman for the Cuban Stars. Dihigo played 12 years in the Negro Leagues. He won three Negro League home-run crowns and tied Josh Gibson for another. As a pitcher, he racked up more than 200 victories in American and Mexican ball.

His versatility as a batter and pitcher drew comparisons to Babe Ruth, who was a star pitcher for the Red Sox before becoming a slugging outfielder with the Yankees. Playing in the Mexican League in 1938, Dihigo batted .387. He also went 18–2 with a 0.90 ERA as a pitcher.

Dihigo left Cuba in protest after Cuban dictator Batista's coup in 1953. He returned to Cuba just days after Fidel Castro's 1959 peasant revolt. Dihigo admired Castro and served as Cuba's minister of sports until his death in 1971.

DiMaggio, Joe

Please see pages 12–13.

Doby, Larry

On July 2, 1947, less than three months after Jackie Robinson integrated the National League, Larry Doby signed with the Cleveland Indians, making Doby the first African-American player in the history of the American League. The left-handed batting, but right-handed throwing, outfielder appeared in only a handful of games in 1947. But by 1949, Doby had made the first of seven straight All-Star Games, becoming one of the A.L.'s top outfielders.

Doby's finest year came in 1954, when his Cleveland Indians posted a record of 111–43. Doby led the American League in home runs and RBI, and finished second to the Yankees' Yogi Berra in MVP voting.

In the middle of the 1978 season, Doby was named manager of the Chicago White Sox, becoming the second African-American manager in big-league history. He was elected to the Hall of Fame in 1998.

Dodger Stadium

Dodger Stadium has been the home of the Los Angeles Dodgers since 1962. The outdoor ballpark is in Los Angeles, California at Chavez Ravine. It is built overlooking downtown Los Angeles and

■ *Dodger Stadium remains one of baseball's loveliest parks.*

the San Gabriel Mountains. It has a well-deserved reputation for being one of the cleanest ballparks in America, and (beginning in 2009, when the Yankees and Mets moved into new digs) is the third-oldest Major League baseball stadium in use, behind only Boston's Fenway Park and Chicago's Wrigley Field.

Walter O'Malley couldn't come to terms with New York on a new stadium for his Brooklyn Dodgers in the mid-1950s, setting into motion the Dodgers' move to Los Angeles. O'Malley found the site at Chavez Ravine, and broke ground on his privately funded stadium in September of 1959.

Dodger Stadium has hosted only one All-Star Game in its 48 seasons (and that was in 1980). But the Stadium has hosted seven World Series.

Dominican Republic, Baseball in

■ *Albert Pujols might be the best Dominican player ever.*

Baseball is an important part of the culture of the Dominican Republic, where the endless summer allows games to be played all year round. The game came to the island in the 1880s, introduced by Cuban immigrants, who had fled their country after the Ten-Year War. They also spread the game throughout the Caribbean islands. Although baseball is often called "America's National Pastime," in the Dominican Republic, where there are hundreds of local teams to follow, *el béisbol* is even more popular and the fans even more enthusiastic than in the United States. In fact, there are more Dominicans playing in the Major Leagues today—about 100—than all other Latin American countries combined.

The Dominican League has attracted many of the best baseball players to the island since the first team was formed in 1895. There are currently six national teams in the Dominican League. Each team begins playing in October, and the 60-game season runs through February. The league champion represents the Dominican Republic in the Caribbean Series to play against the champions of Mexico, Venezuela, and Puerto Rico. In recent years, a great rivalry has developed between two Dominican teams—Los Tigres and Las Aguilas. Each team has won 19 league titles, while Los Tigres has won the Caribbean Series nine times.

Today, many of the league's best players are Major League Baseball players. The first Dominican player to appear in a Major League Baseball game was Ozzie Virgil, an infielder with the New York Giants, in 1956. Since then, more than 400 fellow countrymen, including Hall-of-Fame pitcher Juan Marichal, have lived the dream of playing Major League Baseball. Some of today's biggest stars, including David Ortiz, Robinson Cano, Pedro Martinez, and Albert Pujols, are from the Dominican Republic.

A big moment for national pride came in 2003, when Kansas City's Tony Pena and San Francisco's Felipe Alou became the first Dominicans to manage teams against each other in the Majors. The next year, Omar Minaya was hired by the Mets as the first Dominican general manager.

Doerr, Bobby

Bobby Doerr was a right-handed hitting second baseman who played his entire 14-year career with the Boston Red Sox from 1937 to 1951 (he did not play in 1945). He was a nine-time All-Star, starting at second base for the A.L. five times. He was considered one of the best defensive second baseman of his era. Doerr was a teenager in 1937 when Red Sox scout Eddie Collins signed both Doerr and Ted Williams on the same West Coast scouting trip.

In 1946, the Red Sox won the A.L. pennant. Doerr, who had 116 RBI, finished third in the voting for MVP, trailing only Williams and Detroit's Hal Newhouser.

Following his playing career, Doerr was a longtime coach for the Red Sox. He was voted into the Hall of Fame by the Veterans Committee in 1986.

Double

A hit on which the batter reaches second base safely; also known as a two-bagger. Hall-of-Famer Tris Speaker is the all-time leader with 792 career doubles. The record for most doubles hit in one season is 67, held by Earl Webb, who set the mark in 1931. The current Major Leaguer who is a doubles machine is Todd Helton of the Colorado Rockies. He became the first player in Major League history to hit at least 35 doubles in 10 consecutive seasons. He did it from 1998 to 2007.

■ *The infielder is throwing to first to complete a double play.*

Doubleheader

When the same two teams play two games on the same date. Also called a "twin bill." Most Major League teams do not schedule doubleheaders anymore, but they are used to make up rained-out games.

Double Play

When two outs are made by the defense during one play. Known by the offense as a "twin killing" and by the defense as the "pitcher's best friend."

Most double plays begin at second base, usually on ground balls hit to infielders.

(An "around-the-horn double play goes from third to second to first.) They can also occur on fly balls if the outfielder throws out a runner trying to advance.

Draft, Baseball

Baseball's first amateur draft was held in 1965. The Kansas City Athletics made Arizona State outfielder Rick Monday the No. 1 selection. The amateur draft was renamed the First-Year Player Draft in 1988. Teams use the draft to add players.

Teams select players in reverse order of their previous season's finish, with the American and National Leagues alternating the first pick in even and odd numbered years. The draft is designed to give weaker teams the first crack at selecting the best young players. The players chosen can be graduating high school seniors, junior college players, or college players following their junior years.

Drysdale, Don

Don Drysdale was a big (6-foot-6/ 1.7 m) right-handed pitcher with the Brooklyn and Los Angeles Dodgers for 14 seasons beginning in 1956. The man known as "Big D" won 209 games as the right-handed partner of left-hander Sandy Koufax on the Dodgers' pitching staff throughout the 1960s. Koufax and Drysdale were so vital to the Dodgers' punchless attack in the mid-60s that they teamed up in contract negotiations. The two pitchers were among the first Major League players to bring lawyers and agents to the bargaining table.

Drysdale is best remembered for pitching six consecutive shutouts in 1968. Drysdale didn't allow a run over 58.2 innings, a record that stood for 20 years, when another Dodgers' pitcher, Orel Hershiser, broke the record with 59 scoreless innings.

Never afraid to brush back hitters, Drysdale plunked 154 batters in his career, which remains a National League record for most hit batsmen. Also not afraid to dig in himself, Drysdale was one of the best hitting pitchers in baseball history. He hit 29 home runs in his career, second only to Warren Spahn (35 home runs) among National League pitchers.

Drysdale's best season was 1962, when he led the N.L. in wins, strikeouts, and innings pitched, and won the Cy Young Award. But the Dodgers may have leaned too heavily on him and Koufax. Both burned out young, with Koufax finished in 1966 at the age of 30 and Drysdale in 1969 at the age of 32. Beginning with the 1962 season, Drysdale started 205 games in a

five-year stretch and averaged 310 innings pitched in those seasons.

Following his playing career, Drysdale remained in the public eye, mainly as a television analyst. In 1984, he was inducted into the Baseball Hall of Fame. Two years later, he married Ann Meyers, a member of the Basketball Hall of Fame. Drysdale suffered a heart attack and died at the age of 56 in 1993.

■ *Standout pitcher Don "Big D" Drysdale.*

Duffy, Hugh

Using an unusual batting style in which he choked up very far on the bat, Hugh Duffy was one of the best hitters of the late 1800s. His .438 average in 1894 is among the highest ever recorded. He also had 10 straight seasons with an average of .300 or better (1889–1898). Duffy was a brilliant defensive outfielder, too. He played most of his career with Boston of the National League and was elected to the Hall of Fame in 1945.

Dugout

The covered seating area where players and coaches sit while not on the playing field. Also known as the bench. Players return to the dugout when their team is at bat. There they can rest, get a drink of water, or meet with coaches.

During a game, players store their bats, helmets, and other gear in racks at one end of the dugout. Dugouts are also connected to the clubhouse, where players dress and keep extra gear (and where they can use

■ *Chicago Cubs' player Kerry Wood sits in the dugout during a game.*

the bathroom if they have to). In most stadiums, players walk down a few steps to reach the dugout floor, which by game's end is a sloppy mess that includes empty paper cups and sunflower-seed shells.

Durocher, Leo

Leo Durocher was a shortstop who played for the Yankees, Cardinals, Cubs, and Dodgers from 1925 to 1945. He played on two of the most storied teams of all time, the Yankees' "Murderers' Row" and the Cardinals' "Gashouse Gang." Yet it was as a manager that he became one of baseball's immortals. Durocher was a fiery manager and was credited with the saying, "Nice guys finish last."

Durocher managed in New York, first with Brooklyn and later with its archrivals, the New York Giants, from 1939 to 1955, with the exception of 1947. That year, he was suspended by baseball commissioner Happy Chandler for his "association with known gamblers."

It was with the Giants that Durocher had his greatest success, piloting New York in 1951 past his former Brooklyn team in a three-game playoff that decided the pennant. The Giants won the pennant on Bobby Thomson's famous home run called "The Shot Heard 'Round the World." But the Giants lost in the World Series.

In 1954, Durocher led the Giants to a four-game sweep in the World Series over

■ *Here's Durocher from his playing days.*

the Cleveland Indians, giving "Leo the Lip" his only World Series championship as a manager.

Durocher returned to manage the Chicago Cubs from 1966 to 1972 and the Houston Astros in 1973. Durocher won more than 2,000 games as a Major League manager in 24 seasons with four franchises.

He passed away at the age of 86 in 1991. Three years later, he was voted by the Veterans Committee into the Baseball Hall of Fame.

Earned Run Average

Earned run average, or ERA, is a statistic that measures the number of earned runs that a pitcher allows every nine innings. (An "earned run" is a run that scores without the help of an error, a passed ball, or interference. Runs that score with the help of those plays are not considered

> ### HOW TO CALCULATE ERA
>
> IN THIS EXAMPLE, THE PITCHER HAS ALLOWED 7 EARNED RUNS IN 20 INNINGS OF WORK:
>
> 7 (EARNED RUNS) X 9 = 63
>
> 63 DIVIDED BY 20 (INNINGS) = 3.15
>
> THE PITCHER'S ERA IS 3.15.

■ *Eck was a good starter and dominant closer.*

the fault of the pitcher and are not charged against him and his ERA.)

ERA is a valuable measure of a pitcher's effectiveness—even better than wins and losses, which are often dependent on timing, luck, and the hitting ability of his teammates.

The statistic is calculated by multiplying the number of earned runs allowed by nine, then dividing by the number of innings pitched (see box). The result is carried out two places beyond the decimal point. Any ERA below 4.00 is considered good; an ERA below 3.00 is considered excellent.

Eckersley, Dennis

Dennis Eckersley was a pretty good starting pitcher beginning in 1975, then was converted to the bullpen midway through his 24-season career. The move made him an all-time star. The sidewinding pitcher known as "Eck" went on to become one of the best closers in Major

■ *This photo shows pregame batting practice at Brooklyn's Ebbets Field.*

Ebbets Field

Ebbets Field was the home of the Brooklyn Dodgers from 1913 until the club moved to Los Angeles after the 1957 season. The ballpark was named for Dodgers owner Charles Ebbets. He paid for the ballpark by selling half the franchise in 1912.

The Dodgers' home was noted for its unique dimensions and odd places. For instance, kids could watch games for free by peering through a gap in a metal fence in right-center field. The right-field wall and a protruding scoreboard reportedly produced 289 different angles. It had colorful outfield advertising signs. A well-known one for a men's clothing store read, "Abe Stark: Hit Sign, Win Suit."

Ebbets Field was home to nine National League pennant-winning Dodgers' teams, including the 1955 squad that brought Brooklyn its lone World Series championship. The ballpark was demolished in 1960, and many in the New York City borough still miss this classic old ballpark. An apartment complex was built on the site.

League Baseball history, and he earned induction into the Hall of Fame in 2004.

Eck was only 20 when he first came up to the Cleveland Indians as a rookie in 1975. Two years later, he pitched a no-hitter against the California Angels. He was traded to Boston in 1978 and won 20 games for the Red Sox that year. In 1982, he was the American League's starting pitcher in the All-Star Game.

Eckersley's effectiveness as a starter began to fade, however, and in 1987, the Oakland Athletics made him a reliever. The next year, he saved a league-leading 45 games. In 1992, he saved 51 of the A.L. West-champion Athletics' 96 victories. He was named the league's MVP, as well as the Cy Young Award winner.

As a reliever, the right-handed Eckersley's sidearm delivery, combined with a terrific slider, made him brutally tough on opposing batters, especially right-handers. Despite his late start in the bullpen, his 390 career saves ranks fifth in big-league history.

Error

An error is an official baseball statistic. A defensive player is charged with an error when he physically misplays the ball—usually by missing it, dropping it, or throwing it away. Errors are charged when a misplay allows the offensive team to score a run, advance a base, or extend an at-bat (as in the case of a dropped foul pop-up). Wild pitches and passed balls are not errors. Errors are decided strictly on the judgment of the official scorer.

■ *Oops! This third baseman has dropped the ball for an error.*

■ *With two World Series titles (1997 and 2003), the Florida Marlins are a successful expansion team.*

Expansion

Expansion refers to the addition of new franchises to Major League Baseball. The American League's Tampa Bay Rays and the N.L.'s Arizona Diamondbacks were the last two expansion teams. They joined the big leagues in 1998.

From 1901 (the first season of the American League) through 1960, there was no expansion; both the A.L. and the N.L. played with eight franchises. In 1961, the American League expanded to 10 teams, and in 1962, the National League followed suit. Additional expansion seasons in 1969, 1977, 1993, and 1998 brought the number of franchises to its current total of 30.

Extra Innings

Extra innings are any innings played beyond the regulation nine innings. They occur only when a game is tied at the end of nine innings. After that, play continues until the visiting team has more runs at the end of a complete inning or until the home team goes ahead in its half of the inning.

The longest extra-inning game in Major League Baseball ended in a tie. After 26 innings of a National League game in 1920, Brooklyn and Boston had to settle for a 1–1 tie because it was too dark to continue. In 1984, the Chicago White Sox beat Milwaukee 7–6 in 25 innings, the longest game in A.L. history.

■ *Faber set several records for the White Sox.*

Faber, Red

Red Faber was a right-handed pitcher who won 254 games with the Chicago White Sox from 1914 to 1933. He was elected by the Veterans Committee into the Hall of Fame in 1964.

Faber won 24 games in 1915 and was a 16-game winner in 1917, when the White Sox defeated the Giants in the World Series. Faber won three games in the World Series. He was a member of the 1919 White Sox (infamously known as the "Black Sox") but was injured and didn't play in the World Series. If Faber, who was not touched by the gamblers or the ensuing scandal, had been healthy, manager Kid Gleason wouldn't have relied so heavily on his two tainted aces, Lefty Williams and Eddie Cicotte. Williams and Cicotte started six of the eight Series games, going 1–5.

In 1920, baseball outlawed the spitball but allowed existing spitball pitchers (including Faber) to use the pitch for the remainder of their careers. Faber won 23, 25, and 21 games in the first three years of the 1920s. He retired in 1933, the next-to-last legal spitballer after Burleigh Grimes, who made his last appearance in 1934.

Fair Territory

Any part of the playing field within the baselines and inside the outfield walls.

Fan

A person who roots for a particular team and supports that team during good times and bad.

Fantasy Baseball

A game that allows a person to act as general manager of his or her own team, and to compete against other fans' imaginary teams. Fans select real Major

League players for their fantasy teams and score points based on the real-life statistical performances of the players. Most leagues are conducted on the Internet with paid services keeping track of all the statistics for the fantasy leagues.

Fastball

A straight pitch that is thrown with great speed and power. A fastball pitcher with a great "heater" is said to be "throwing smoke." Also called high cheese.

Federal League

The baseball business was booming in the early 1910s. With hopes of joining in the fun, the eight-team Federal League was established in the winter of 1913. The new league immediately began buying star ballplayers from the National and American Leagues. Chicago Cubs' shortstop Joe Tinker and Cincinnati Reds' pitcher Mordecai "Three-Finger" Brown were two of the first to jump to the new league. Walter Johnson, the Washington Senators' legendary fastball pitcher, nearly signed with the upstart league, but at the last moment the American League owners chipped in to pay for a salary increase for "The Big Train."

On April 13, 1914, one day before Major League Baseball's Opening Day, the Federal League launched its inaugural season as the Baltimore Terrapins beat the Buffalo Feds 3–2 in front of 27,140 fans.

Some Federal League players shined during the inaugural season. Benny Kauff paced the league with a .370 batting average for the Indianapolis Hoosiers, who captured the Federal League flag in 1914.

Fans, however, soon returned to watching the established American and National League teams. Federal League teams struggled to sell tickets and lost money. The league folded after the 1915 season. An agreement was negotiated between the Federal League and Major League Baseball, in which the N.L. and A.L. owners paid each of the Federal League owners $600,000. The American and National

■ *The Chicago Whales were in the Federal League.*

27

Feller, Bob

Using a blazing fastball and knee-buckling curveball, Bob Feller became one of the most intimidating pitchers in baseball in the 1930s and '40s. Indeed, "Rapid

■ *Feller was just 17 when he joined Cleveland.*

Robert" was one of the greatest right-handed pitchers ever. His 266 career victories, an impressive number, would have been even better if he hadn't lost years in the prime of his career to military service.

Feller, born on an Iowa farm in 1918, credited his childhood chores with strengthening his arm. He was signed by the Cleveland Indians following 10th grade. Teams weren't allowed to sign high school players then, so Cleveland kept him hidden from other franchises, breaking another rule. However, he was allowed to stay with the Indians.

Feller made his first Major League start in August 1936 when he was just a teenager. The 17-year-old struck out 15 batters. In September, he tied the A.L. single-game record with 17 strikeouts. The next year he led the American League in strikeouts with 240, and in 1939, at age 21, he became the youngest pitcher ever to win 20 games in a season. (He would hold that record as the youngest for almost 50 years, until Dwight Gooden beat the feat in 1984).

Feller will forever be remembered for Opening Day, 1940. He pitched a 1–0 no-hitter against the White Sox. It is still the only no-hitter on Opening Day. In 1941, Feller won 25 games and finished third behind Joe DiMaggio and Ted Williams in the MVP voting.

At the end of 1941, Feller was just 23 years old and yet had compiled 107 big-

■ *Feller still visits many ballparks.*

league victories. But when Feller heard about the Japanese invasion of Pearl Harbor on December 7, he decided to put his Major League career on hold. He immediately signed up to serve in the Navy, and missed four seasons because of World War II.

He returned to the Major Leagues in 1946 and pitched a third no-hitter. That was his career-best season, when he finished with 26 wins, a 2.18 era, and a then-record 348 strikeouts. Feller was elected to the Hall of Fame in 1962 and remains a beloved figure in Cleveland.

League owners agreed to forgive those players that had jumped to the Federal League, and allowed them to be reinstated.

Two Federal League owners were allowed to purchase existing Major League teams. Charles Weeghman took over the Chicago Cubs, and Philip Ball took control of the St. Louis Browns.

All of the Federal League teams abided by the agreement except for one. The Baltimore franchise pursued a lawsuit all the way to the U.S. Supreme Court. The result was a 1922 decision by Justice Oliver Wendell Holmes that gave Major League Baseball the ability to operate without competition. The American and National Leagues had become the first professional leagues to successfully eliminate an upstart rival. The judge's ruling continues to give baseball a unique way to operate its business as 30 competing groups that can band together to keep new teams from forming without their permission.

Fehr, Donald

Donald Fehr has been the executive director of the Major League Baseball Players Association for more than two decades, beginning in 1986. The MLBPA is a union, a group of people that work in the same industry who band together to try to create good working conditions for all.

Fehr has been a bulldog for the players, helping them sign contracts worth millions

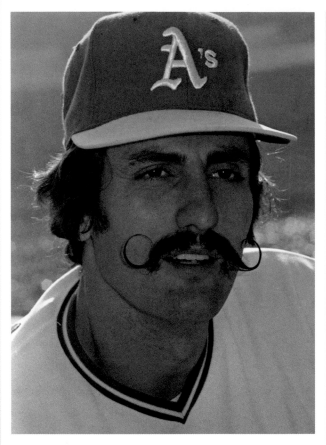

■ *Fingers shows off his famous mustache.*

and millions of dollars. In the late 1980s, the owners colluded in an attempt to prohibit free agency. This meant that they had illegally agreed among themselves to pay the players less. Companies, or teams, can't join forces like that, according to business laws. Fehr helped the players get a $280 million payment from the owners for this rule-breaking.

Fehr's union has been called the strongest in professional sports, and possibly the strongest union in the country. Since 2005, Fehr has been criticized—along with baseball management and the media—for ignor-

ing the growing issue of the use of illegal steroid drugs in baseball. George Mitchell's report in early 2008 (see "Mitchell Report") spread the blame, but included Fehr's group as one party to the problem.

Feller, Bob
Please see pages 28–29.

Fielder's Choice
Occurs when a fielder catches a batted ball and instead of making the out on the batter decides to try to make an out on a baserunner instead.

Fielding Percentage
This is a statistic that measures the rate a defensive player successfully fields a batted or thrown ball. Fielding percentage is calculated by adding putouts and assists, and dividing that number by the number of total chances handled by the fielder.

Fingers, Rollie
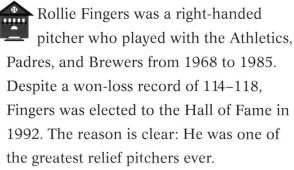Rollie Fingers was a right-handed pitcher who played with the Athletics, Padres, and Brewers from 1968 to 1985. Despite a won-loss record of 114–118, Fingers was elected to the Hall of Fame in 1992. The reason is clear: He was one of the greatest relief pitchers ever.

A seven-time All-Star, Fingers was a big part of the Oakland A's dynasty that won three straight World Series championships

Fenway Park

Fenway Park, home of the Boston Red Sox since 1912, is the oldest baseball ballpark still in use. The park's name comes from the Fens, a marshy area of the city where the park was built. It was originally built as a one-deck brick ballpark taking up a city block. As a result, its unique shape is different than any other ballpark.

The left-field wall is known as "The Green Monster." It stands 37 feet (9.8 m) high and was created in 1947. Originally, it was covered by ads, but they were removed, and the wall was painted green. A 23-foot (7-m) screen was added above the wall to keep home-run balls from flying into the street.

In 1940, in an effort to help Red Sox slugger Ted Williams hit more home runs, the Red Sox added the right-field bullpens, known as Williamsburg, which reduced the distance to the fence by 23 feet. One seat in the right field bleachers is painted red, marking the spot where the longest home run ever hit by a Red Sox player landed. Williams hit the home run 502 feet in 1946.

The most famous home run hit in Fenway came in Game Six of the 1975 World Series. A television camera inside the wall of the Green Monster caught Boston's Carlton Fisk waving his extra-inning, game-winning home run fair.

The Red Sox aren't the only team to call Fenway Park home over the years. The Boston Braves played World Series games there in 1914, as their stadium was being renovated. The NFL's Boston Redskins (who later moved to Washington) used Fenway as their home stadium for four years beginning in 1933. The Boston Patriots (now known as the New England Patriots) played their AFL games there from 1963 to 1968.

■ *The "Green Monster" in left field dominates Fenway Park.*

from 1972 to '74. He was the MVP of the 1974 World Series against the Dodgers. Fingers was at his best in the biggest situations. In 33 World Series innings, he allowed only five runs for a 1.35 ERA.

In the prime of Fingers' career, closers were used much differently than today. Now, closers are just used for one inning. In rare cases, top relievers are needed to get four or five outs for a save. But in the mid-1970s, it was very different. In 1975, for example, Fingers pitched in 75 games and worked 127 innings. He had a 10–6 record, meaning he was brought into tie games, unlike today's closers, who usually only protect a lead. In 1976, Fingers had 24 decisions (13–11) and pitched more than 134 innings despite not starting a game.

■ *Fisk slaps a tag on a sliding runner.*

Following the 1976 season, Fingers signed with the San Diego Padres. He played four seasons with the Padres, and four with the Brewers. He won the Cy Young Award and the Most Valuable Player award with Milwaukee in 1981. Fingers is also remembered for a handlebar mustache, which he grew after Oakland owner Charles Finley offered players $300.

At the time of Fingers' enshrinement in Cooperstown, he was only the second relief pitcher to be voted into the Hall, following Hoyt Wilhelm. Since Fingers, Bruce Sutter, Dennis Eckersley, and Goose Gossage have also been elected.

First Baseman

A defensive player who is positioned on the right side of the infield near first base. Also called the "first sacker."

Fisk, Carlton

Carlton Fisk, who was known as "Pudge," wore both White Sox and Red Sox uniforms during a 24-year career. He was one of the best catchers ever. At the time of his retirement, no catcher ever played more games (2,226) or hit more home runs (360).

Fisk won the Rookie of the Year award in 1972 with the Red Sox, and was fourth in the MVP voting that year. Fisk will forever be remembered

■ *To catch most fly balls, the fielder runs to where the ball will land and catches it above his head.*

for winning Game Six of the 1975 World Series with a home run in the 12th inning. Not even a loss in Game Seven could make Sox fans forget Game Six against the Reds, a game many still call the greatest ever.

Following the 1980 season, a Red Sox executive was late in mailing out a contract to Fisk, making him a free agent. Fisk rejected a later Red Sox offer, and signed with the White Sox. He played with Chicago for 13 years—longer than he played for Boston. Fisk hit 72 home runs after the age of 40. Fisk was elected to the Hall of Fame in 2000.

Flood, Curt

Please see pages 34–35.

Florida Marlins

Please see pages 36–37.

Fly Ball

A ball hit high in the air. If a defensive player catches a fly ball hit by a batter in either fair or foul territory, the batter is out. Fly balls that don't travel too far into the outfield are also called popups and are often caught by infielders. Most fly balls are caught by outfielders, though.

Flood, Curt

Curt Flood was an All-Star center fielder for the St. Louis Cardinals from 1958 to 1969. He batted .300 or better in six seasons, and won seven consecutive Gold Glove Awards for fielding excellence. Flood was the team captain of the 1967 World Series-champion Cardinals.

Following the 1969 season, however, the Cardinals tried to trade Flood to the Philadelphia Phillies. But Flood didn't want to play in Philadelphia. He wrote a letter to Commissioner Bowie Kuhn saying that his trade from the Cardinals to the Phillies should be voided and that he should be made a free agent.

"After twelve years in the Major Leagues," he wrote, "I do not feel I am a piece of property to be bought and sold irrespective [regardless] of my wishes. I believe that any system which produces that result violates my basic rights as a citizen and is inconsistent with the laws of the United States.

"It is my desire to play baseball in 1970, and I am capable of playing. I have received a contract offer from the Philadelphia club, but I believe I have the right to consider offers from other clubs before making any decision. I, therefore, request that you make known to all Major League Baseball clubs

■ *A solid all-around player, Flood gained his fame in court.*

my feelings in this matter, and advise them of my availability for the 1970 season."

Kuhn replied that baseball would hold Flood to the provisions in his contract, which included the Cardinals' right to trade Flood to any team. Flood sought an injunction (a court ruling) that would prevent baseball from invoking its "reserve clause" rules against him, but his request was denied. Flood announced that he would retire from baseball rather than report to the Phillies.

Flood filed a lawsuit against Major League Baseball in January 1970, charging baseball with violation of the antitrust laws. These laws cover most businesses and prevent them from doing what baseball was doing. At 31 and in the prime of his career, Flood chose to sit out the 1970 season to pursue his case. It reached the U.S. Supreme Court in July 1972. The court voted 5–3 against Flood.

Although he lost in court, Flood's suit had exposed a big problem in baseball. By the end of the year, the team owners brought an end to the reserve clause. They agreed to let an outside observer called an arbitrator make decisions on salaries, choosing between numbers suggested by players and owners.

Flood sacrificed his career to make a point. His action is considered by many to be brave and a key moment in labor relations. Flood died at age 59 in 1997.

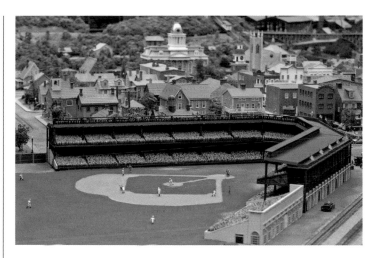

■ *This handmade model shows Forbes Field.*

Forbes Field

Forbes Field was the home of the Pittsburgh Pirates from 1909 to 1970. Its enormous outfield distances produced fewer home runs than most ballparks, but many more triples.

There were still many memorable home runs hit there. In May 1935, while playing for the Boston Braves, Babe Ruth hit the first home run ever to travel over the Forbes Field roof in right field. Ruth hit three homers on that day–Nos. 712, 713 and 714–a few days before he retired.

The biggest home run ever hit in Forbes Field was by the Pirates' Bill Mazeroski, whose "walk-off" home run ended the 1960 World Series. In that Series, the Pirates defeated the mighty New York Yankees in seven games. Forbes Field was the Pirates' home for more than a half century, yet 1960 is one of just four World Series

continued on page 38

Florida Marlins

The Marlins began play in 1993, and the club won a pair of World Series championships in its first 11 years. Florida won both titles as a wild card. In 1997, the Marlins' fifth season, they became the first wild-card team to win the World Series.

When the Marlins hired former Pittsburgh manager Jim Leyland before the 1997 season, he inherited a very good pitching staff

■ *Ivan Rodriguez helped Florida win in 2003.*

headed by Al Leiter and Kevin Brown. The Marlins then added third baseman Bobby Bonilla and outfielder Moises Alou.

In 1997, Alou and Bonilla teamed to drive in 211 runs. Combined with an excellent pitching staff and a solid defense, the Marlins won 92 games to finish nine games behind the division-winning Braves.

In the postseason, Florida swept San Francisco. That set up the National League Championship Series against Atlanta.

The Marlins and Braves split the first two games in Atlanta. In Miami for the third game, a 22-year-old rookie named Livan Hernandez outdueled Greg Maddux, a certain future Hall of Famer. Atlanta tied the series 2–2 with a shutout in the fourth game. In the pivotal fifth game, Marlins ace Kevin Brown was sick and unable to pitch, forcing Leyland to give the ball to Hernandez, who had defected from Cuba just two years earlier. Hernandez pitched a complete game three-hitter and struck out 15 Braves as Florida won 2–1. In the sixth game, the Marlins scored four in the top of the first inning, and Brown went the distance to advance Florida into the World Series.

The Marlins were three outs away from losing the World Series to the Indians. Craig Counsell's sacrifice fly in the bottom of the ninth of Game Seven tied the game at 2–2. Then, with the bases loaded and two outs in the bottom of the 11th, Edgar Rentería's soft liner scored Counsell gave the title to Florida.

Despite the championship, the team ownership began breaking up the roster, citing low revenue. The Marlins won only 54 games in 1998. It was the first of five consecutive losing seasons for the Marlins.

In 2003, an old manager (72-year old Jack McKeon) and a young pitching staff (including 21-year-old Dontrelle Willis and 23-year-old Josh Beckett) combined to win 91 games. Florida returned to the postseason as a wild card.

The Cubs led the N.L. Championship Series 3–2 and had a 3–0 lead in the sixth game at Chicago's Wrigley Field. But the Marlins took advantage of some bad breaks against the Cubs and scored eight runs in the eighth inning. Then they won Game Seven to advance to the World Series against the New York Yankees.

In a stunning upset, the Marlins defeated the mighty Yankees in six games to win the World Series for a second time in franchise history.

Once again, the team sold off high-priced players. Yet in 2006, with a payroll of only $21 million dollars, the

■ *Florida's star shortstop Hanley Ramircz.*

Marlins contended for yet another postseason slot under the guidance of rookie manager Joe Girardi. The team was in the pennant hunt until the final days in September. Once again, the Marlins did it with a young pitching staff, as four rookies won at least 10 games.

On February 21, 2008, the city of Miami approved the building of a baseball-only stadium for the Marlins (they had been sharing with the NFL's Miami Dolphins).

The ballpark deal keeps the team in Miami until at least the 2046 season, and the franchise will be renamed the Miami Marlins when the new stadium opens in April of 2011.

FLORIDA MARLINS

LEAGUE: **NATONAL**

DIVISION: **EAST**

YEAR FOUNDED: **1993**

CURRENT COLORS:
TEAL, GREEN

STADIUM (CAPACITY):
**DOLPHIN STADIUM
(42,531)**

ALL-TIME RECORD
(THROUGH 2008):
1,196–1,328

WORLD SERIES TITLES
(MOST RECENT):
2 (2003)

■ *Ford was dominant in the World Series for New York.*

(1909, 1925, 1927, 1960) for the team in that span. Forbes Field was torn down, and the Pirates moved to new Three Rivers Stadium in 1970.

Force Play

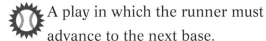 A play in which the runner must advance to the next base.

Ford, Whitey

Edward Charles "Whitey" Ford was the ace of the New York Yankees pitching staff in the 1950s and early '60s. He won 236 games, winning 69 percent of his career decisions—the best of any 20th-century pitcher. He was the American League Cy Young winner in 1961, with a record of 25–4.

Ford is best known for his work in the World Series. He helped the Yankees win eight World Series. Ford won a record 10 World Series games, and once pitched 33 straight scoreless innings in the Fall Classic. Known as "The Chairman of the Board," he allowed only 44 earned runs in his 22 World Series starts.

Ford joined the Yankees in 1950 and he was 9–1, leading the Yankees to the World Series against the Phillies. Ford won the fourth and deciding game of the 1950 World Series, and then was drafted by the Army and missed each of the next two seasons.

In 1954, Ford rejoined the Yankees and became lifelong pals with teammates Mickey Mantle and Billy Martin. Whitey and Mantle would be enshrined in the Hall of Fame together in 1974.

Forkball

A pitch thrown by holding the ball with the first and second fingers spread apart on top and the thumb on the bottom. Forkballs sink sharply because they have little spin on them. Also called a sinker or split-fingered pitch.

Foster, Rube

Andrew "Rube" Foster was an important player, manager, owner, commissioner, and pioneer of the Negro Leagues. Born in 1879, Foster was one of the greatest black pitchers in the early 1900s. It's been written that he got his nickname from besting the great pitcher Rube Waddell in 1902.

The greatest manager in black baseball in the segregated days began as player-manager in 1907 of the Leland Giants. In 1910, he formed a dynasty of sorts with his Chicago American Giants. By February of 1920, the 41-year old Foster, then the owner and manager of the American Giants, called a meeting of influential African-American baseball men in Kansas City. He decided to form his own baseball league, known as the Negro National League, with him as president as well as retaining his titles as owner and manager of the American Giants.

The barnstorming league thrived in the 1920s, with Foster's American Giants and the Kansas City Monarchs being the best teams and attractions.

In 1926, Foster began a period of decline in his mental state and was institutionalized. On December 9, 1930, he died in a mental hospital. The Negro National League disbanded and fell apart that same year.

For his contributions to baseball, Foster was elected to the Hall of Fame in 1981.

Foul Ball

Any batted ball that lands in foul territory outside the baselines. Foul balls can be caught on the fly for an out. The first two foul balls in an at-bat are strikes. Other foul balls do not count against the batter.

Foul Pole

A long pole situated on both foul lines at the base of the outfield wall that helps umpires decide if batted balls are a home run or a foul ball. A batted ball striking the foul pole on the fly is a home run. For this reason, many people believe it should be called a fair pole.

■ *The tall yellow pole in the background is the foul pole.*

Foul Territory

 Any part of the playing field outside of the baselines. A batted ball that lands in this area is foul, and counts as strike one or strike two, but not strike three (unless it is bunted into foul territory).

Foul Tip

A ball that is just barely grazed by the bat and then is caught directly by the catcher, or bounces right at the batter's feet. A foul tip caught by a catcher on the fly can be recorded as a third strike.

Foxx, Jimmie

Jimmie Foxx was one of the greatest right-handed sluggers in baseball

■ *Thanks to his name, Foxx was called "Ol' Double X."*

history. He belted 534 home runs, which at the time of his retirement, ranked him second in career home runs to Babe Ruth.

In 1932, Foxx hit 58 home runs, two shy of Ruth's single-season record. But Foxx had hit two more homers that season in games that were rained out and weren't counted. Foxx played in the era of the Great Depression, and his Philadelphia Athletics salary actually went down after 1933, when he batted .356 and hit 48 home runs. Before the A's had to be broken up for economic reasons, Connie Mack's team won consecutive A.L. pennants in 1929, 1930, and 1931 (winning the World Series the first two of those seasons).

Foxx was the MVP in 1932 and 1933, and won the Triple Crown in 1933. In 1935, Foxx was sold to the Boston Red Sox. He nearly won another Triple Crown in 1938 with Boston.

Foxx was sold to the Cubs in June of 1942, retiring after the season. In 1943, Cubs owner William Wrigley named Foxx manager of one of the teams in the new All-American Girls Professional Baseball League. The 1991 film, *A League of their Own*, is based on these teams. The manager in the movie, Jimmy Dugan, played by Tom Hanks, is based on Foxx.

Foxx was elected into the Hall of Fame in 1951. He died in 1967 at the age of 59.

Free Agent

A player whose contract with his current team has expired, allowing him to take his services to the team of his choosing, usually to the highest bidder. Free agency only began in Major League Baseball in the 1970s. Free-agent salaries have risen steadily since.

Frisch, Frankie

Frankie Frisch played 19 seasons in the Major Leagues, the first eight with the New York Giants and the final 11 with the St. Louis Cardinals. He was one of the greatest second basemen of all time, and one of the best switch-hitters.

Known as "The Fordham Flash" while attending Fordham University in New York, Frisch was a star with the Giants, leading them to World Series titles in 1921 and 1922, and National League pennants in 1923 and '24. He was one of the best basestealers, batters, and fielders of the decade. But his relationship with legendary Giants manager John McGraw soured. Following the 1926 season, Frisch was traded for Cardinals superstar Rogers Hornsby in one of baseball's biggest trades ever.

Frisch won the MVP award in 1931 and led the Cardinals to a World Series triumph. Two years later, he became the team's player-manager. In 1934, St. Louis won the World Series, Frisch's fourth title in seven trips to the Fall Classic.

■ *Hall-of-Fame second baseman Frankie Frisch.*

Frisch also managed the Pirates and Cubs before retiring with a lifetime batting average of .316 to go along with 419 career stolen bases. He was elected to the Baseball Hall of Fame in 1947.

Fungo

A fly ball hit during practice to give fielders a workout. Coaches use a thin-handled "fungo bat" to hit these balls. The origin of the term "fungo" is obscure, and no one is really sure where it came from.

41

Gaedel, Eddie

Eddie Gaedel was a 3-foot 7-inch (1 m) circus performer who appeared in a Major League game for the St. Louis Browns on August 19, 1951. Gaedel, wearing a tiny Browns uniform with the number 1/8 on the back, walked on four pitches and was pinch-run for. He is the shortest player in Major League history.

His one and only appearance was the idea of Browns owner Bill Veeck, who was famous for his crazy stunts. Veeck signed Gaedel to an official contract. He made sure Browns manager Zach Taylor had a copy, in case the umpiring crew questioned whether Gaedel was really a player. Then, Gaedel was announced as the pinch-hitter for Browns' lead-off batter Frank Saucier in the bottom of the first inning. Manager Taylor brought out the official A.L. contract with Gaedel's signature on it, and the umpires had no choice but to allow Gaedel his turn at bat.

Gaedel, who was told by Veeck not to swing the bat, looked at four straight balls from Tigers pitcher Bob Cain, and ran to first base, where he was replaced by pinch-runner Jim Delsing. Within two days, the

■ *A tiny strike zone helped Eddie Gaedel walk in his one and only big-league at-bat in 1951.*

rules were changed to ban special, one-time players such as Gaedel from the game. However, to this day, Eddie Gaedel's name is on the list of Major League Baseball players—if only for one at-bat.

Gagne, Eric

Eric Gagne was the dominant relief pitcher in the National League for a three-year stretch beginning in 2002. Pitching for the Dodgers, the Canadian-born Gagne saved 52 games in 2002, 55 games in 2003, and 45 games in 2004. He set a record by converting 84 consecutive save opportunities in a span of the 2002 and '03 seasons. Gagne was the Cy Young Award winner in 2003, when he had a miniscule 1.20 earned run average.

Arm injuries plagued him for much of the 2005 and '06 seasons. After signing a free-agent contract with the Texas Rangers, Gagne was traded late in the 2007 season to the Boston Red Sox. He pitched ineffectively, but won a ring when the Sox swept the World Series. He joined the Milwaukee Brewers in 2008.

Gap

The areas between outfielders in left-center field and right-center field are each called "gaps." A line drive hit to left-center field or right-center field that rolls between the outfielders and reaches the fence is called a "gapper."

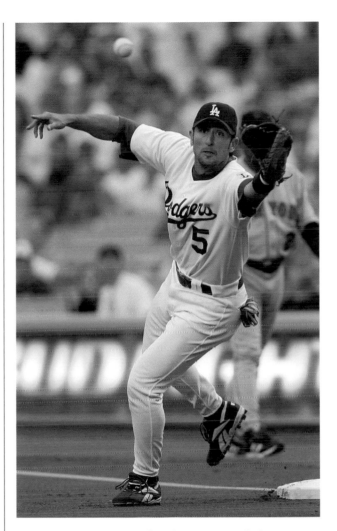

■ *Garciaparra moved to first base in L.A.*

Garciaparra, Nomar

Nomar Garciaparra was one of a trio of excellent young shortstops that appeared on the American League scene during the mid-1990s, along with Alex Rodriguez and Derek Jeter. Garciaparra had a career average of .333 after his first five seasons with the Boston Red Sox, becoming a Fenway Park favorite. He led the American League in hits during his Rookie

continued on page 46

Gehrig, Lou

Lou Gehrig is generally regarded as the greatest first baseman in baseball history. In his career, he hit 493 home runs (including a record 23 grand slams) and had a .340 batting average. Also known as "The Iron Horse," Lou's nickname refers to his re-

■ Gehrig had a powerful, left-handed swing.

markable durability. From June 1, 1925, until May 2, 1939, he played in 2,130 consecutive games, all for the New York Yankees. He was a member of six World Series-winning teams. Unfortunately, his career and his life were cut short and he died in 1941 of a disease of the nerves that later was named for him. The brave and noble way he handled himself amid this tragedy has made him one of the sports world's most beloved figures.

Gehrig was born in New York City in 1903, and never strayed too far from his roots. He attended Columbia University there and signed with the Yankees in 1923. After a handful of games on the Major League level in 1923 and 1924, the left-handed Gehrig pinch-hit on June 1, 1925. He stayed in the lineup the next day, replacing the usual starting first baseman, Wally Pipp. Pipp stayed with the team, but he never recovered his starting job and was traded following the season.

In 1927, Gehrig won the American League Most Valuable Player Award. He batted

.373 with 47 home runs (that was the year Babe Ruth hit 60) and 175 runs batted in. Some experts consider the 1927 Yankees the greatest team of all time. Gehrig batted fourth in the powerful Yankees' batting order (hence, he wore No. 4), protecting Babe Ruth in the lineup (who batted third and was No. 3). They were a terrific tandem for a decade, from 1925 to 1934, but because of Ruth's outsize personality, Gehrig was often overshadowed. When it came to driving in runs, though, Gehrig was a machine. He drove in at least 100 runs for 13 consecutive seasons, and established the American League record with 184 RBI in 1931. On June 3, 1932, Gehrig became the first A.L. player to hit four home runs in a game. In 1934, Gehrig achieved the batting Triple Crown by leading the league in home runs (49), RBIs (165), and batting average (.363).

■ *Gehrig teared up on his "day" in 1939.*

In 1938, Gehrig's numbers began a steep decline. At the time no one knew why. His streak of 2,130 games ended in Detroit on May 2, 1939, when the Yankee captain removed himself from the starting lineup. He would never play again. Soon after, he would learn that he was suffering from amyotrophic lateral sclerosis (ALS, now known as Lou Gehrig's Disease.)

On July 4, 1939, the Yankees honored Gehrig between games of a doubleheader. His illness had recently been made public. Obviously sick, Gehrig told the crowd that "for the past two weeks you have been reading about the bad break I got. Yet, today, I consider myself the luckiest man on the face of the earth." Later that year, Gehrig was inducted into the Hall of Fame. There is usually a five-year wait, but baseball wanted to honor Lou immediately. He passed away on June 2, 1941, at the age of 37.

with the Los Angeles Dodgers in 2006 with his sixth All-Star season. Despite the injuries, Nomar's career average in 12 seasons in the majors was a robust .314 through 2008.

People remember Garciaparra for other things besides his batting titles and All-Star Game appearances. He has a pre-at-bat ritual while preparing for each pitch that includes tugging his gloves and tapping his toes. His unique first name is his father Ramon's name spelled backwards, and he has a famous wife, soccer star Mia Hamm. The two wed in 2003.

Gashouse Gang

■ *Dizzy Dean (dark jacket) and the Gashouse Gang.*

This was the nickname given to the St. Louis Cardinals' team in 1934. When a sportswriter who had asked how the Cardinals would fare against an American League team, shortstop and team captain Leo Durocher reportedly said, "They wouldn't let us play in the American League; they would say we were just a bunch of gashouse players." Back then, a gashouse was located in the seedy part of town, and gashouse workers got dirty and smelly. The Cardinals wore dirty uniforms, and most of their players came from poor backgrounds.

of the Year season in 1997, and was league batting champion in 1999 (.357 average) and 2000 (.372 average).

Much of Garciaparra's power was lost after he suffered a wrist injury in 2001. An Achilles' tendon injury cost him the early months of the 2004 season, the year in which he was traded to the Chicago Cubs in mid-season (and the one that ultimately wound up with Boston winning a World Series for the first time since 1918). Nomar was injured again in 2005, but rebounded

The Gashouse Gang, led by player-manager Frankie Frisch, won the World Series in 1934. They took the pennant by two games over the New York Giants and outlasted the Detroit Tigers in a seven-game World Series triumph. The Cards not only led the National League in victories, but also in colorful nicknames. They had Dizzy (Dean, who won 30 games), Daffy (Dean, Dizzy's brother, who won 19 games), Ducky (Medwick, who batted .319 with 106 RBI), Ripper (Collins, the first baseman who batted .333, with 35 homers and 128 runs batted in), and third baseman Pepper (Martin, also known as the "Wild Horse of the Osage").

Gehrig, Lou

Please see pages 44–45.

Gehringer, Charlie

Charlie Gehringer was a slick-fielding second baseman for the Detroit Tigers for 19 seasons during the 1920s and 1930s. He wasn't flashy, but he was appreciated by his teammates for his all-around skills. A lifetime .320 hitter who batted over .300 in 13 seasons, Gehringer led the Tigers to their first World Series title in 1935, batting .375 in the Series. He was the MVP of the 1937 season after batting a career-best .371, which led the league. When his manager, Mickey Cochrane, was asked to describe the quiet second baseman, he said, "Charlie says hello on Opening Day, goodbye on closing day, and in between hits .350."

Gehringer was elected into the Hall of Fame in 1949.

General Manager

A team executive who is mainly responsible for acquiring players, writing and planning contracts, and hiring a field manager. The team owner or president hires the general manager.

General managers also supervise the team's scouts, who watch high school, college, and pro teams, looking for future players. General managers try to put together the best team of players they can within the owner's budget. Unlike most field managers, many general managers are not former players. A knowledge of business and baseball is important for the "G.M."

■ *Gehringer did his talking with his bat.*

Giambi, Jason

Giambi has been a high-average slugger for two teams, a five-time All-Star, and the 2000 A.L. MVP. The first baseman joined the Athletics in 1995. In his MVP season, he hit 43 homers, drove in 137 runs, and hit .333. He signed a huge free-agent contract to join the New York Yankees in 2002 and helped them reach the playoffs three times, including the 2003 World Series that the Yankees lost to Florida. Giambi is one of only a few players to admit using steroids earlier in his career.

Gibson, Bob

Bob Gibson was one of the most intimidating and successful right-handed pitchers of the post-World War II era. Pitching for the St. Louis Cardinals from 1959 to 1975, Gibson won 251 regular season games, but is best remembered for his World Series dominance.

Gibson led the Cardinals to three pennants and two World Series championships. He was the Most Valuable Player of the 1964 World Series, allowing three runs in 27 innings, and winning the clinching

■ *Bob Gibson was called "The Great Bird" because of the way he "flew" off the mound after a pitch.*

Gibson, Josh

Josh Gibson was considered the greatest slugger ever to play in the Negro Leagues. Many fans in the 1930s thought that Gibson, a catcher, was every bit the slugger that Babe Ruth was. But Gibson wasn't allowed to play in the segregated Major Leagues.

Gibson was born in 1911, and earned a reputation in his teens playing semipro ball. In 1930, Gibson was watching the Homestead Grays play a game. When Grays' catcher Buck Ewing got injured, manager Judy Johnson asked Gibson to suit up. Gibson stayed with the Grays for four years, and then jumped to the Pittsburgh Crawfords, where he played with Satchel Paige.

The Negro Leagues did not keep reliable statistics, but in his 13 seasons, Gibson is said to have won nine home-run titles and four batting crowns. He hit an estimated 800 home runs for his career. Regardless of the numbers, nobody hit the ball farther than Gibson. He is credited with clouting the longest home runs ever hit in Pittsburgh's Forbes Field, Cincinnati's Crosley Field, and New York's Yankee Stadium.

In late 1942, doctors discovered that Gibson had a brain tumor. Refusing an operation, Gibson returned to play baseball, battling headaches and dizziness. That season,

■ *Was Josh Gibson baseball's best catcher?*

he won another batting title. Then, from 1944 to 1946, he led the Negro Leagues in home runs each season.

Although he was still relatively young when baseball integrated, the years of hard living and the rigors of catching an untold number of innings, made Gibson old before his time. He might also have been battling effects of drug abuse and alcoholism. Unfortunately, Gibson did not live to see Jackie Robinson break the color barrier with Brooklyn. He died before the 1947 season opener, at 35 years old.

Tom Glavine won his 300th career game in 2007.

er Curt Flood misplayed a fly ball into a three-run eighth inning for Detroit. Gibson's 35 total strikeouts were also a single-Series record.

In his nine World Series starts, Gibson was 7–2, with eight complete games. His postseason earned run average was 1.89, and he struck out 92 batters and walked only 17.

Gibson was so determined and competitive that after a 1967 start in which he was struck by a batted ball that broke his leg, he remained on the mound to finish the inning. In 1968, Gibson had one of the greatest seasons in history. On his way to winning the Cy Young Award and the MVP award, he had a record of 22–9, including 15 straight wins, with 13 shutouts. He finished the season with a 1.12 earned run average (the lowest ever by a pitcher with at least 300 innings pitched).

Game Seven. He was MVP of the 1967 World Series, again winning Game Seven. In leading the Cards to the title, he went 3–0, pitching three complete games and recording an ERA of 1.00.

In the 1968 Series, he defeated 30-game winner Denny McLain 4–0 in Game One and set a Series record by striking out 17 Tigers. He bested McLain again in Game Four, 10–1. In Game Seven, though, he lost 4–1 to Mickey Lolich as Cardinals outfield-

The Cardinals' ace won a second Cy Young Award in 1970. When he retired following the 1975 season, he was only the second pitcher to reach 3,000 strikeouts in his career, and was the first to fan 200 or more in a season nine times. A former member of basketball's Harlem Globetrotters, Gibson was a great athlete, winning nine Gold Glove Awards and hitting 24 home runs in his career. He was a first-ballot Hall of Famer in 1981.

Glavine, Tom

Tom Glavine has been one of baseball's best left-handed pitchers since 1987. Pitching for the Atlanta Braves and New York Mets, he has started nearly 700 games, which ranks among the all-time leaders. He has won more than 300 games in his career, and he earned Cy Young Awards in 1991 and 1998.

Teaming with John Smoltz and Greg Maddux, Glavine was part of the pitching trio that helped lead the Braves to 14 straight division titles beginning in 1991. Glavine has been the starting pitcher in 35 postseason games. He will forever be remembered in World Series history for his work against the Cleveland Indians in the sixth and deciding game of the 1995 Fall Classic. Glavine allowed only one hit in eight innings while striking out eight batters, and the Atlanta Braves won the game 1–0 and the Series championship.

Glove

A fielder's most important piece of equipment, the glove is worn by a defensive player to catch and field batted or thrown balls. Gloves are usually made of leather or cowhide. Fielders' gloves have only been used since the 1870s. Early baseball players used fingerless pads for their palms, and gloves gradually grew in size over the years. Catchers and first baseman use special gloves (which can be called "mitts") that are shaped to help them do their jobs, such as scooping low throws or pitches out of the dirt.

Gold Glove Award

The award presented by the baseball glove maker Rawlings since 1957. Gold Gloves are given to one player in each league at each infield position, with three awards given in each league for outfielders with no distinction made for right, center, or left field. Pitcher Greg Maddux holds the record for most Gold Glove Awards (17) See page 85 for more Gold Glove records.

■ *This fatter, less-laced glove is from the 1930s.*

Grand Slam

A home run with the bases loaded. In slang, also called a "grand salami."

"Grand-Slam Single"

A grand-slam single is technically not possible because a grand slam is a home run. However, the term has become

■ *Pete Gray lost his right arm in a farm accident.*

part of baseball lore. It famously occurred on October 17, 1999, when the New York Mets defeated the Atlanta Braves in 15 innings in Game Five of the NLCS. In the game, the Braves scratched out the go-ahead run in the top of the 15th inning. The Mets tied the game in the bottom of the inning and had the bases loaded. Robin Ventura hit a ball over the fence—a grand slam—to give the Mets an apparent 7–3 victory. However, Ventura was mobbed by his Mets' teammates and never made it past first base. Umpires ruled that the 15-inning game had ended after 5 hours and 13 minutes with a final score of 4–3 Mets.

Grapefruit League

Term given to spring training games played in Florida, because of one of that state's most famous fruit crops. By contrast, spring training games played in Arizona are called Cactus League games. Teams prepare for the regular season during spring training. As of 2008, eight teams were based in Florida, with the rest based in Arizona. The Dodgers planned to move to Arizona from Florida beginning in 2009.

Gray, Pete

Pete Gray played 77 games in the outfield for the St. Louis Browns in 1945. He did this without a right arm, which had been amputated following a childhood accident. Gray played in a time (the early 1940s) when the country needed young men to fight in World War II. But Major League Baseball kept playing (see "Green-Light Letter") and used men, young and old, who couldn't qualify for the military. None drew as much attention as the one-armed rookie Pete Gray.

Gray batted .218 in his 234 at-bats, which worked out to 51 hits, including eight for extra-bases, and 13 runs batted in. His greatest day as a big leaguer occurred on May 19, 1945, when he collected five hits in a doubleheader at Yankee Stadium.

Gray was naturally right-handed, but after the accident he had to learn how to do everything with his left arm. He would catch a ball in his mitt, flip the ball in the air, drop the mitt, then grab the ball and throw it in. He swung the bat with his one arm. He was also a very speedy baserunner. His presence on a big league ball field was an inspiration to all disabled people, and especially to those injured veterans who had returned home from military duty.

■ *Greenberg was the first prominent Jewish ballplayer.*

Greenberg, Hank

Hank Greenberg was one of the greatest right-handed power hitters in history. He played only about nine full seasons because of World War II military service, but he pounded out 331 home runs. If he hadn't missed most of the 1941 through 1945 seasons, he might have had a shot at reaching the lofty 500-home-run mark.

Griffey, Ken Jr.

 No one seems to have more fun playing baseball than Ken Griffey Jr. He has combined awesome power, great defensive skills, and a joyful attitude throughout his career.

The player known as "Junior" made it to the Majors with the Seattle Mariners in 1989. At age 19, he was the youngest player in the Major Leagues. He made an immedi- ate impact on Mariners' fans, ripping a home run on the very first pitch he ever saw in the Kingdome in his first at-bat in front of the home crowd.

Ken grew up around baseball. His father, Ken Griffey Sr., played for the 1975 and 1976 World Series-champion Cincinnati Reds, and other teams, during his 19-year career. In 1990, he was still playing when Junior made the bigs, and in 1990, the two were reunited on the Mariners. They became the first father

■ *Griffey played for Cincinnati starting in 2000. He joined the White Sox during the 2008 season.*

and son to play Major League Baseball together on the same team when they took the field against the Kansas City Royals, on August 31, 1990. Two weeks later, on September 14, 1990, they became the first father and son to hit back-to-back homers!

In 1993, at age 23, Griffey smashed 45 home runs. In July of that season he homered in eight consecutive games, tying the Major League record. As good as Ken was with the bat, he was even better with the glove. He won the Gold Glove Award each year from 1990 to 1999. His ability to snatch back an apparent home run or snag a line drive on the dead run became a regular highlight on the nightly news.

In 1995, Griffey's postseason heroics helped save baseball in Seattle. According to mid-September polls, a proposal to increase the state sales tax to pay for a new ballpark would be soundly defeated. But the measure passed after Griffey scored the winning run in a playoff over the Yankees. That victory remains Griffey's only postseason triumph.

Griffey was the American League Most Valuable Player in 1997, and became the youngest member of the All-Century team in 1999. Following that season, he forced a trade to his hometown Cincinnati Reds, where his father had enjoyed so much success. In July 2008, however, Cincinnati traded him to the Chicago White Sox.

Greenberg was an outfielder and first baseman for the Detroit Tigers in the 1930s and '40s, leading the Tigers to four pennants. He was the first great Jewish baseball player and much admired for his determination to succeed despite discrimination and religious intolerance. But Greenberg kept his cool and answered the bigots with his bat. In fact, he claimed that the slurs only motivated him to play better. "I came to feel that if I, as a Jew, hit a home run, I was hitting one against Hitler."

His religion became a huge storyline in the final days of the 1934 season, when in the middle of a pennant race he chose not to play on Yom Kippur, which is the holiest day on the Jewish calendar. The Tigers lost the game, but reached the World Series, losing to the Cardinals.

In 1938, Greenberg took aim at Babe Ruth's single-season home run record. He had 58 homers—two shy of Ruth's record—with five games left to play. But Greenberg wouldn't hit another out of the park. Some say anti-Semitic (which mean anti-Jewish) pitchers wouldn't give him anything good to hit, but Greenberg downplayed this theory.

He was the American League MVP in 1935 and 1940, but the Tigers lost the World Series both times. He enlisted in the Army in 1941, and when he returned to the Tigers in July 1945, he hit a home run in his first game back. The Tigers were on the verge of a final-week collapse, and

■ *Here's Fenway Park's Green Monster decorated in honor of the 1999 All-Star Game.*

needed Greenberg's dramatic grand slam in the season finale to nail down the 1945 American League title. Greenberg slammed two homers and drove in seven runs to lead Detroit to a seven-game World Series victory over the Cubs.

In 1947, the Pittsburgh Pirates made Greenberg the first player to earn an annual salary of $100,000. He retired following that season, and was elected to the Hall of Fame in 1956.

Green-Light Letter

In 1941, the United States entered World War II. Hundreds of thousands of American men joined the military to fight in the war, including many players in pro baseball. Some people thought that baseball should stop playing during the war, because the players were gone and people would be busy helping at home. However, in 1942, President Franklin Roosevelt wrote a letter to the baseball team owners suggesting that baseball continue to be played. Roosevelt felt that baseball would give hard-working people a break and would help continue some sort of normal life, even as the nation turned its energies to war. This letter is known as the Green-Light Letter because it gave baseball the "go" signal to keep playing. Although many top players joined the military, all the teams found younger, older, or less-fit players to keep their games going.

Green Monster

Nickname given to the 37-foot-high (9.8-m) left-field wall at Boston's Fenway Park. It is the highest outfield wall in the Major Leagues, and boasts one of the last remaining hand-operated (as opposed to electronic) scoreboards. The wall was built during the ballpark's original construction in 1912, but the nickname was coined in 1947, the year the wall was painted green.

Griffey, Ken Jr.

Please see page 54.

Griffith Stadium

Griffith Stadium was the home of the Washington Senators until 1960, when they moved to Minnesota and became the Twins. An A.L. expansion team, also called the Senators, played at Griffith Stadium in 1961. The stadium was also the home of the Negro Leagues' Homestead Grays. Griffith Stadium was the home of the NFL's Washington Redskins, too. They played there from 1937 to 1960.

In 1910 at Griffith Stadium, President William Howard Taft started a tradition by throwing out the first ball on Opening Day.

Grimes, Burleigh

Burleigh Grimes was the last of the legal spitball pitchers. Known as "Old Stubblebeard" for his custom of not shaving on the days he pitched, he won 270 Major League games in a career that started in 1916 with Pittsburgh. He often used a spitball, which meant that he put spit, grease, dirt, or other stuff on the ball, making it spin or move in odd ways. In 1920, the pitch was outlawed, but players who were already using it were allowed to keep using it until the end of their careers. Grimes was the last of this group to retire.

Grimes threw the last "legal" spitball in 1934. Grimes pitched 19 years, hurling for

■ *Grimes pitched for the Cardinals in 1931.*

six N.L. clubs, then closed out his playing career with a brief stint with the Yankees. Along the way, Grimes won N.L. pennants with the Dodgers in 1920, the Cardinals in 1930 and 1931, and the Cubs in 1932. He won his only World Series in 1931 at the age of 38, going 2–0 with a 2.04 ERA in the Fall Classic for the Cards.

Ground Ball

A ball hit on the ground; also called a grounder. In slang, also called a "grass-cutter" or a "worm-burner." A high-bouncing ground ball that goes for a base hit is called a "Baltimore chop."

Ground-Rule Double

When a batter is awarded two bases on a hit that lands in fair territory and bounces over a fence or is interfered with by fans.

Grounds Crew

A group of stadium or team workers who care for the baseball field itself, before, during, and after games. The crew prepares the infield dirt and cuts the outfield grass, makes sure the field is watered, and covers it in bad weather. It puts the lines on the field, install bases, and make sure the pitcher's mound is set up properly.

■ *To keep the dirt smooth, the grounds crew drags the infield between some innings of most games.*

Grounds-crew members come on the field between innings to pull metal screens around the infield dirt, smoothing it and helping to prevent bad hops or bad footing. If rain develops, they quickly roll out large field coverings.

Grove, Lefty

Robert Moses "Lefty" Grove was the greatest left-handed pitcher in American League history. He led the American League in strikeouts seven times, led in ERA a record nine times, led in victories four times, and led in win percentage five times. His lifetime record was 300–141 for a .680 winning percentage and a 3.06 ERA.

Born in 1900, Grove won more than 100 games for the Baltimore Orioles in the International League in the early 1920s. He didn't reach the big leagues until he was 25 years old in the spring of 1925, when he joined the Philadelphia Athletics.

Grove was the ace of the Athletics' staff for their pennant winning teams from 1929 to 1931, compiling a 79–15 record over that time. The Athletics won the pennant each of those years and the World Series in 1929 and 1930. In 1931, with offensive numbers at an all-time high, Grove had perhaps the best season ever for a pitcher. He won the Most Valuable Player award with a record of 31–4, including 17 straight wins and an earned run average of just over two runs per game.

■ *Guerrero is enjoying a Hall-of-Fame career.*

In 1933, Grove's contract was sold to the Boston Red Sox. He won more than 100 more games until retiring in 1941. He was elected to the Hall of Fame in 1947.

Guerrero, Vladimir

Vladimir Guerrero made his Major League debut as a teenager late in the 1996 season with the Montreal Expos (now Washington Nationals). From the beginning, the right fielder from the Dominican Republic showed off an outstanding throwing arm, running speed, and the ability to hit for high average and power. He is known as the best bad-ball hitter in the Majors (meaning he can often hit

■ *Guidry was known as "Louisiana Lightning."*

Guidry, Ron

Ron Guidry was the ace of the New York Yankees' pitching staff in the late 1970s and early '80s. "Louisiana Lightning" and "Gator" were two popular nicknames for the left-hander who won 170 games between 1975 and 1988.

Guidry had his greatest season in 1978, when he won the Cy Young Award with an eye-popping 25–3 record, including nine shutouts and a 1.74 earned run average. He started and won the tie-breaker to determine the A.L. East division title winner on just two days of rest at the end of the season at Fenway Park in Boston. Earlier that season he had struck out 18 California Angels batters in a game, beginning the Yankee Stadium tradition of fans methodically clapping for a strikeout whenever the batter gets two strikes against him.

A power pitcher with a blazing fastball and a darting slider that belied his wiry frame, Guidry overcame arm trouble in 1981 to win 21 games in 1983 and 22 games in 1985. He served as a Yankees' co-captain from 1986 to '89, and had his jersey No. 49 retired in 2003.

Gwynn, Tony

Tony Gwynn of the San Diego Padres was the best hitter in the National League for most of two decades. He played right field for 20 years, was voted to the All-Star team 15 times, and retired after the

pitches out of the strike zone), and is one of the few hitters remaining who doesn't use batting gloves. An outstanding athlete, "Super Vlad," as he is known, has been a league-leader in a wide number of categories, including home runs, stolen bases, runs scored, and hits. Guerrero signed a free-agent contract with the Angels before the 2004 season and took the American League by storm, leading the Angels to the postseason and winning the MVP award.

Guerrero has a lifetime batting average of .323 through the 2008 season and has been an eight-time All-Star. He is one of a dozen players in history to hit their 300th career home run before their 30th birthday.

2001 season with a career average of .338. Only Ty Cobb and Nap Lajoie got their 3,000th hit faster than Gwynn. Gwynn finished his career with 3,141 hits. He was elected to the Hall of Fame in 2007.

Gwynn won eight National League batting titles, and finished second once and third twice. A student of hitting, he was one of the first players to study his batting stance and swinging motion by watching video tapes of his previous at-bats. This combination of modern technology and old-fashioned hard work paid off. Gwynn's batting average was above .300 for 19 consecutive seasons. He was really in a hitting groove against San Francisco on August 4, 1993, getting six hits in that one game.

In 1994, many experts thought Gwynn would become the first batter since Ted Williams in 1941 to reach the vaunted .400 average for a season, but his batting average was frozen at .394 when owners locked out the players on August 11, 1994, ending that season early.

Gwynn led the Padres to the franchise's first World Series appearance in 1984, a five-game loss to the Detroit Tigers. Gwynn made the most of his return to the Series 15 years later. In the 1998 World Series, the 38-year old Gwynn batted .500 against the Yankees, but the Padres were swept by New York in four games.

Gwynn remains in baseball as the head coach at San Diego State University (his alma mater). He can also enjoy watching his son, Tony Jr., who plays for the N.L.'s Milwaukee Brewers.

■ *The perfect swing gave Gwynn 3,141 career hits.*

Haddix, Harvey

Harvey Haddix was a three-time All-Star pitcher who won 136 games in 14 big-league seasons from 1952 to 1965. But he will always be remembered for one night in 1959 when he turned in one of the most incredible pitching performances in baseball history.

On May 26 that year, while pitching for the visiting Pittsburgh Pirates, Haddix set down the Milwaukee Braves in order for 12 consecutive innings—36 batters in a row without one reaching base. Unfortunately, his teammates couldn't push across a run off Milwaukee pitcher Lew Burdette. Finally, in the 13th inning, a Braves' hitter reached base on a throwing error to lead off the inning, breaking up Haddix's perfect game. After a sacrifice bunt and a walk, Milwaukee's Joe Adcock won the game by drilling a ball over the fence. The no-hitter and the game were lost, too. (Adcock's hit eventually was ruled a double, and the final score was 1–0 because the runner on first base, Hank Aaron, left the basepath before scoring.) Still, no pitcher before or since ever has taken a perfect game into extra innings.

Haddix made his Major League debut with St. Louis late in 1952 and won 20 games for the Cardinals in his official rookie season in '53. He also pitched for the Philadelphia Phillies and Cincinnati Reds before joining the Pirates in 1959. He closed his career with two seasons for the Baltimore Orioles beginning in 1964.

■ *Hafner's power bat from the left side has helped the Tribe fly.*

Hafner, Travis

Travis Hafner is the left-handed, power-hitting designated hitter for the American League's Cleveland Indians. In 2006, he equaled the Major League record for grand-slam home runs in a season with six.

Hafner originally was drafted by the Texas Rangers

in the 31st round in 1996. He made his big-league debut with that team in 2002, but was traded to the Indians before the next season. In 2004, he batted .311 for Cleveland and drove in more than 100 runs (109) for the first of four years in a row. Hafner's career bests for home runs and RBI came in 2006, when he belted 42 round-trippers and drove in 117 runs. That was the same year that he tied former Yankees slugger Don Mattingly's record of six grand slams. Hafner occasionally plays first base when he is not serving as the Indians' DH.

Halladay, Roy

Roy Halladay is the ace starting pitcher for the Toronto Blue Jays. He was the American League's Cy Young Award winner for 2003. The keys to his success are pinpoint control and a fastball with lots of movement on it.

Toronto selected the right-hander with the 17th overall pick of the 1995 amateur draft, and he made his Major League debut with a couple of late-season starts just three years later at the age of 21. He won 19 games and posted an ERA of 2.93 in 2002 to earn the first of his four career All-Star selections. Then he had his best season the next year, going 22–7 with a 3.25 ERA and 204 strikeouts in 266 innings pitched to earn the A.L.'s top pitching honor. Roy also won 16 games in back-to-back seasons in 2006 and 2007.

■ *Halladay is one of the A.L.'s top righties.*

Halladay's given first name is Harry (Roy is short for Leroy, his middle name). His nickname is "Doc."

Hamilton, Josh

Hamilton is one of the feel-good stories in baseball in recent seasons. In 1999, Hamilton was chosen as the first overall pick of the amateur draft by Tampa Bay. He seemed destined for a great, long career. However, during his early minor-league years, he was derailed by drug use. Hamilton struggled with his addictions for several years, until finally overcoming them

Henderson, Rickey

Few baseball experts would argue against calling Rickey Henderson the greatest leadoff hitter in big-league history. For 25 seasons beginning in 1979, he was a thorn in the side of opposing pitchers and catchers with his aggressive baserunning skills. But he also showed uncharacteristic power for a leadoff man, and belted 297 home runs and drove in 1,115 runs in his career. He was a lifetime .279 hitter, but his on-base percentage was .401.

Henderson's accomplishments are impressive. He scored more runs (2,295) and stole more bases (1,406) than anyone else in baseball history. Only Barry Bonds drew more walks, and only Bonds, Pete Rose, and Ty Cobb reached base more often. Henderson was a 10-time All-Star, played in the postseason eight times, and was on World Series champions in both Oakland and Toronto.

Henderson led the American League in steals 11 times in 12 seasons from 1980 to 1991, including 1982, when he set a big-league record by swiping 130 bases. His best overall season came in 1990, when he batted .325 with 28 home runs and 65 steals to earn league MVP honors for the A.L.-champion A's.

Amazingly, Henderson kept on playing until he was 44 years old. At 39 in 1998, he led the A.L. with 66 stolen bases while playing for the A's. Henderson last played in the big leagues with the Los Angeles Dodgers (his ninth big-league team) in 2003. He is eligible for induction into the Hall of Fame in 2009.

■ *Henderson was a threat to score every time he hit.*

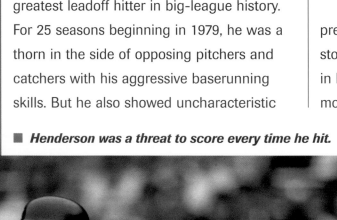

with the help of family and friends. He returned to baseball and finally made it to the Majors in 2007 with Cincinnati. Traded to Texas, he exploded in 2008, reaching 100 RBI by midseason, while also belting 30 homers. He put on a memorable show at the All-Star Game Home Run Derby, whacking 32 homers in an early round. Hamilton looks finally ready to fulfill his early promise.

Helton, Todd

Five time All-Star first baseman Todd Helton spent his 12th season with the Colorado Rockies in 2008. He was the National League's batting champion for 2000.

Todd was a quarterback in football as well as a baseball star at the University of Tennessee in the mid-1990s. The Rockies selected him with the eighth overall pick of the 1995 draft, and he was in the big leagues by 1997. He hit .315 in his first full season in 1998 and did not bat below .300 until an injury-shortened 2008 season.

Helton, who belted his 300th career homer in 2007, has hit as many as 49 round-trippers in a season (2001). His best overall season came in 2000, however, when he hit 42 home runs. His .372 average that year was the best in the National League, and he also topped the circuit in on-base percentage (.463), slugging percentage (.698), and RBI (147) that season. Helton holds many of the Rockies' career

■ *Helton is one of the top hitters of the 2000s.*

batting records, including the marks for hits, runs, home runs, and RBI. He also is an outstanding fielder who has earned three Gold Glove Awards during his career.

Hernandez, Felix

Hard-throwing right-hander Felix Hernandez is one of the most promising young pitchers in baseball today. He is a starter for the American League's Seattle Mariners.

Hernandez is a native of Venezuela who signed with Seattle when he was just 16 years old. By the time he was 19, he was

■ *Prince Fielder shows how to get a hit.*

in the big leagues. He won 12 games in his first full season as a starter in 2006, then went 14–7 with a 3.92 ERA in '07.

"King Felix" can throw his fastball 100 miles per hour, but he also has a nasty curve and an effective slider. The Mariners believe that he can become one of baseball's best pitchers in the very near future.

Hernandez, Livan

Just two years after fleeing Cuba, Livan Hernandez was thrust into the international baseball spotlight. After finishing second in the 1997 Rookie of the Year voting for the N.L., the young right-hander took

charge as the Florida Marlins advanced through the playoffs to reach the World Series in only their fifth season. Hernandez won two games against the Braves and was the Series MVP.

Hernandez spent four seasons with Florida and has since moved on to pitch for the Giants, Expos/Nationals, Diamond-backs, Twins, and Rockies.

Hernandez, Orlando

Orlando, known as "El Duque," was already a superstar pitcher for the national team in his native Cuba when he decided to seek greener pastures. He traveled by a small boat with other defectors, arriving in Costa Rica in 1997. He signed to play for the Yankees and by 1999 was the MVP of the ALCS. Hernandez was a key part of the Yanks' rotation for three seasons. He moved to the White Sox and Diamond-backs before pitching for the Mets.

Hit

Hit is most commonly used as a noun and refers to the statistical category of the same name. A hit is awarded for any batted ball that allows the batter to reach base safely without the benefit of a mistake by the fielding team. Most hits are obvious, but sometimes the official scorer must make a decision on whether the batter reached base because of a hit or because of an error by the fielder.

Hit also can be used as a verb. In that case, it can mean taking a turn at bat, or making contact with any pitched ball. In other words, a batter can "hit" the ball and get a "hit." But he can also "hit" the ball and make an out.

Hit-and-Run

The hit-and-run is a strategic play in which a baserunner (usually on first base) begins running as soon as the ball is pitched and the batter is instructed to swing at the pitch no matter where it is. (On a run-and-hit play, the batter has the option of swinging or not.)

One of the benefits of a hit-and-run is that it is more difficult for the defense to turn a double play if the ball is hit on the ground at an infielder. Another benefit is that it puts the fielders in motion (one of them must cover the base to which the runner is going), which gives the batter a gap in the field he would not normally have. Also, the runner usually can move up an extra base on any hit that reaches the outfield.

There are downsides to the hit-and-run, though, too. If the batter swings and misses, the runner is at risk for being thrown out by the catcher at the next base. Or if the batter hits a line drive that is caught by a fielder, the runner is usually too far from the previous base to return safely, and the defense can get an easy double play.

Hit for the Cycle

A batter that hits for the cycle in a game has at least one of each of the four types of base hits: a single, double, triple, and home run. The hits can come in any order (although a player that gets them in order is said to hit for a "natural cycle").

Hitting for the cycle is rare, but not impossible. In 2007, for instance, three Major League batters hit for the cycle. Three big-league teams—the Florida Marlins, San Diego Padres, and Tampa Bay Rays—have never had a player hit for the cycle.

Hitting Streaks

A hitting streak is the number of consecutive games in which a player gets a base hit. Hitting streaks do not end if a player does not play in a game or is not credited with an official at-bat (for instance, he draws a walk or sacrifices in his only plate appearance).

Former Yankees great Joe DiMaggio holds the record for the longest hitting streak at 56 games, which he did in 1941. It is one of the most famous records in sports, and one that many baseball fans believe will never be broken. See chart on page 68.

Hoffman, Trevor

Relief pitcher Trevor Hoffman is Major League Baseball's all-time saves leader. He closed the 2009 season, his 17th in the big leagues, with 554 career saves.

STREAKS!

The following big-league players have had a hitting streak of 35 games or more:

GAMES	PLAYER	TEAM	YEAR
56	JOE DIMAGGIO	New York (AL)	1941
44	WILLIE KEELER	Baltimore (NL)	1897
	PETE ROSE	Cincinnati	1978
42	BILL DAHLEN	Chicago (NL)	1894
41	GEORGE SISLER	St. Louis (AL)	1922
40	TY COBB	Detroit	1911
39	PAUL MOLITOR	Milwaukee (AL)	1987
37	TOMMY HOLMES	Boston (NL)	1945
36	JIMMY ROLLINS	Philadelphia (NL)	2005
35	FRED CLARKE	Louisville (NL)	1895
	TY COBB	Detroit	1917
	LUIS CASTILLO	Florida	2002
	CHASE UTLEY	Philadelphia (NL)	2006

■ *DiMaggio's streak: unbeatable?*

All but two of Hoffman's saves have come while with the San Diego Padres, which he joined in 1993.

Hoffman soon established himself as the Padres' closer—and as one of the best in the game. In 1998, he led the National League by posting 53 saves. He earned the first of six career All-Star selections that year and finished second in the balloting for the National League's Cy Young Award.

Hoffman topped the league again and was the Cy Young runner-up in 2006, when he posted 46 saves. That year, he also surpassed Lee Smith at the top of baseball's all-time saves list.

Hole

A hole can refer to any gap between players on the infield. Most commonly, though, "the hole" refers to the gap between the shortstop and the third baseman on the left side of the infield. It takes a strong-armed shortstop to throw out a batter who is running to first base after he has hit the ball into the hole.

Home Plate

Home plate is the five-sided, hard rubber slab that is the destination for any runner on the basepaths. Crossing home plate after safely reaching each of the other three bases produces a run for the player's team. That's how score is kept in baseball.

Home plate also is the target for a pitcher's pitches and the place off to the side of which the batter stands. To be called a strike without the batter swinging, a pitched ball must cross any portion of the plate and be in the imaginary rectangle formed by a batter's knees and his armpits (although, in reality, most umpires call a strike zone that is smaller than that).

Home plate is 17 inches wide at the top end (facing the pitcher) and 17 inches deep. It is shaped like a rectangle with a triangle attached to the bottom (in other words, a pentagon). The back end (facing the catcher) comes to a point and determines the foul lines. Home plate itself is in fair territory.

■ *The rubber home plate is buried in the infield dirt.*

THE BIG FLY GOES YARD

There are lots of different nicknames for a home run (page 70). Here are just a few of them:

BIG FLY	HOMER
BLAST	JACK
BOMB	KNOCK
CIRCUIT CLOUT	LONG BALL
DINGER	MOON SHOT
FOUR-BAGGER	ROUND-TRIPPER
GONE YARD (VERB)	TATER

Homer in the Gloamin'

The "Homer in the Gloamin'" is a famous round-tripper slugged by the Chicago Cubs' Gabby Hartnett in 1938. Hartnett's blast was the key to Chicago's pennant that year. "Gloamin'" is slang for the darkness just before sunset.

The Cubs and the Pittsburgh Pirates were in a tight pennant chase late in 1938. On September 28, the two teams met in Chicago's Wrigley Field. The Pirates led the Cubs by half a game entering that day, and the game turned out to be as tight as the pennant race: The teams entered the bottom of the ninth inning tied 5–5.

With darkness descending, the umpires decided to call the game after

■ *"The Rajah" is one of the all-time greats.*

nine innings if the score was still tied. The first two Cubs went down in order, then Hartnett fell behind Pittsburgh relief pitcher Mace Brown no balls and two strikes. Hartnett took a mighty swing at Brown's next pitch and drilled it through the darkness and into the left-field bleachers. Chicago won 6–5.

Hartnett's homer enabled the Cubs to edge past the Pirates into first place in the standings. Chicago beat Pittsburgh in a rout the next day and went on to win the pennant by two games.

Home Run

A home run is a batted ball on which a player crosses all four bases on one hit. This usually means he has hit a long, fair fly ball over the fence. In rare instances, a batter can cross all four bases on one hit that doesn't go over the fence and without the aid of a fielding error. That's called an "inside-the-park home run."

Barry Bonds is Major League Baseball's all-time leader with 73 home runs in one season (2001) and 762 home runs in his career. Hank Aaron (755) and Babe Ruth (714) are the only other players to top the 700 mark in their career, while Mark McGwire (70 in 1998) is the only other player to hit 70 home runs in a season.

Hornsby, Rogers

Rogers Hornsby was one of the greatest hitters in Major League history—some call him the greatest right-handed hitter ever. The second baseman batted .358 in 23 seasons from 1915 to 1937. His average is second only to Ty Cobb's .366 mark on baseball's all-time list.

"The Rajah" hit .370 for the St. Louis Cardinals in 1920 to win the first of six consecutive N.L. batting titles. After finishing second in 1927, he was back on top for the seventh time in '28.

Hornsby played his first 12 years with the Cardinals. He batted .424 in 1924—the second-highest single-season mark in the 20th century—and .403 in 1925. That year, he won his second N.L. Triple Crown (leading the league in home runs, RBI, and batting average in the same season) and earned the first of his two MVP awards.

Hornsby was inducted into the National Baseball Hall of Fame in 1942, and was named to Major League Baseball's All-Century Team in 1999.

Hot Corner

The hot corner is a nickname for third base and its surrounding area. It's "hot" because balls hit toward third base often comes off the bat and at the third baseman very quickly.

■ *Third baseman Mike Lowell prepares to field a hard-hit ground ball as he plays the "hot corner."*

Houston Astros

The Houston Astros have been very successful since joining the N.L. Central in 1994. They are still looking for a World Series championship, however.

The Astros began their existence as the Houston Colt .45s in 1962. They played at Colt Stadium in Houston. Houston, along with the New York Mets, who also joined the N.L. that year, were the first N.L. expansion teams added in the 20th century. Houston took a while to build a winner.

■ *The Astros celebrate their 1980 division title.*

After three seasons of 90-plus losses, the club got a new home in 1965—and a new nickname because of it. The team moved into the Houston Astrodome that year. It was the first large, domed stadium in the world.

The Astrodome got its name because of Houston's importance to the space program, and the Astros got their name because of their new home. (After the first year, the field in the Astrodome featured the world's first artificial grass, nicknamed AstroTurf.)

Unfortunately, the new ballpark didn't translate to more wins. Good players included infielder Joe Morgan (who would go on to Hall-of-Fame success with the Cincinnati Reds), outfielder Jimmy Wynn, and pitcher Larry Dierker. But the team did not win more games than it lost until 1972. That year, 21-year-old center fielder Cesar Cedeno blossomed into an All-Star for the first time, and the Astros were the surprise team of the National League, finishing second in the N.L. West.

The Astros made the playoffs for the first time in 1980. With no-hitter king and strikeout ace Nolan Ryan joining a staff that also included 20-game winner Joe Niekro and J.R. Richard, Houston rode its strong pitching to the division championship. The West was decided with a one-game playoff victory over the Dodgers. However, Houston lost to the Phillies in an exciting NLCS.

The Astros made the playoffs a couple more times in the 1980s, including 1986, when Ryan and Cy Young winner Mike Scott were a formidable one-two pitching duo. The team's hitters included first baseman Glenn Davis and outfielder Kevin Bass. This time, the Mets stopped Houston, winning the NLCS-deciding game in 16 innings.

The Astros joined the National League Central when that division was formed in 1994. Houston finished in first or second place in its new division every year but one through the 2006 season. In 2000, the team moved out of the Astrodome into new Minute Maid Park. The new stadium has a retractable roof—that means it can open or close depending on the weather—and a real grass field.

In the late 1990s and early 2000s, the Astros became known for their lineup

of "Killer Bs": first baseman Jeff Bagwell, outfielder Lance Berkman, and second baseman and outfielder Craig Biggio. That trio helped Houston win the division title for the fourth time in five seasons in 2001. Each time, however, the playoffs produced disappointment.

■ *Slugging Astro Lance Berkman.*

Finally, in 2005, the Astros made it to the World Series for the first time. Young third baseman Morgan Ensberg (36 home runs and 101 RBI) picked up the slack on offense.

Veterans Roger Clemens and Andy Pettitte teamed with 20-game winner Roy Oswalt on the pitching staff. After earning a wild-card playoff spot, Houston first beat the Braves, then the Cardinals to win the N.L. pennant. The season ended with a World Series sweep at the hands of the A.L.-champion Chicago White Sox, but that could not spoil the first league pennant—finally—in the Astros' history.

HOUSTON ASTROS

LEAGUE: **NATIONAL**

DIVISION: **CENTRAL**

YEAR FOUNDED: **1962**

CURRENT COLORS: **NAVY BLUE, BURNT ORANGE, AND PALE YELLOW**

STADIUM (CAPACITY): **MINUTE MAID PARK (40,950)**

ALL-TIME RECORD (THROUGH 2008): **3,738–3,747**

WORLD SERIES TITLES: **NONE**

Hot Stove League

The Hot Stove League isn't a league at all. Rather, it's the talk about baseball—trade rumors, signings, prospects, and second-guessing—during the winter months in the offseason. (In the old days, that might mean baseball fans getting together around the hot stove of a barber shop, country store, or other community gathering place.)

Houston Astros

Please see pages 72–73.

■ *The big lefty Howard is one of baseball's best home-run hitters.*

Howard, Ryan

Ryan Howard is the first baseman for the Philadelphia Phillies. He was the N.L.'s rookie of the year in 2005, and was the league MVP in 2006.

The left-handed slugger made his big-league debut in September of 2004, then hit 22 home runs after a mid-season callup the next year. He really broke out in '06, blasting a club-record 58 home runs while batting .313. From 2006 through 2008, he hit more homers and drove in more runs than any other player. He helped the Phillies win the 2008 World Series.

Hubbard, Cal

Cal Hubbard is the answer to a trivia question: Who is the only man to be in both the baseball and football Halls of Fame?

Hubbard is in the baseball Hall for his role as an umpire. He was an American League umpire for 16 seasons beginning in 1936, and worked in four World Series and three All-Star Games. He was listed at 6 feet 5 inches and 250 pounds in his football playing days, and that imposing size made him an authoritative umpire. So did his keen vision, which once was measured at 20–10 (which is even better than 20–20 "normal" vision).

Before becoming an umpire, Hubbard was a two-way tackle in the National Football League from 1927 to 1933 and 1935 to 1936, mostly with the Green Bay Packers and New York Giants. He earned all-league honors six times, and was a charter member of the Pro Football Hall of Fame in 1963. In 1976, he was elected to the National Baseball Hall of Fame.

■ *Great athlete, great ump: Cal Hubbard.*

Hubbell, Carl

Carl Hubbell was a Hall-of-Fame pitcher who won 253 games for the New York Giants from 1928 to 1943. He amassed 115 of those victories in a dominating five-year span of the 1930s, during which time he twice was named the National League's most valuable player.

The best pitch thrown by "King Carl" was a screwball, which breaks the opposite direction of a curveball. It's a hard pitch to throw, with the pitcher twisting the wrist sideways as he releases the ball. Hubbell mastered the tricky pitch and used it to earn nine All-Star selections and help the Giants to three N.L. pennants. He pitched a no-hitter in 1929, and won 24 consecutive decisions in a span of the 1936 and 1937 seasons.

The left-handed Hubbell is perhaps best known, however, for his performance in the 1934 All-Star Game. In that contest, he struck out five future Hall-of-Fame sluggers in a row: Babe Ruth, Lou Gehrig, Jimmie Foxx, Al Simmons, and Joe Cronin. Ruth, Gehrig, and Foxx all went down in the same inning!

■ *Yankees manager Miller Huggins stands between his two stars: Babe Ruth (left) and Lou Gehrig.*

Huggins, Miller

Miller Huggins was the Hall-of-Fame manager of the powerful New York Yankees' teams of the 1920s. He guided his "Murderer's Row" teams to six American League pennants and three World Series titles in the decade.

Huggins was a big-league infielder for 13 seasons, and he became the player-manager of the National League's St. Louis Browns near the end of his active career in 1913. After five unremarkable seasons at St. Louis' helm, he took over in New York in 1918. Two years later, the Yankees acquired pitcher and outfielder Babe Ruth from the rival Boston Red Sox.

Huggins made Ruth almost exclusively an outfielder, and the slugger became the centerpiece of the most intimidating lineup in baseball. New York won the first of three consecutive pennants in 1921, capped by its first World Series title in '23. In 1926, the team began another string three pennants in a row, with the 1927 and 1928 teams combining to win 211 regular-season games and the World Series each year.

Hulbert, William

National League fans can thank Chicago businessman William Hulbert for the league they enjoy today. Hulbert was the owner of the Chicago franchise of the National Association, which had started in 1871. He was unhappy with the NA, however, as several owners were less-than-honest, and the play was very rowdy. To combat this, in 1876 Hulbert formed the National League. He was later league president. For his contributions, he was named to the Hall of Fame in 1995.

Hunter, Catfish

Catfish Hunter won 224 games in 15 seasons from 1965 to 1979. He also made a lasting impact on the business of baseball as one of the first big free agents.

Hunter helped the Oakland A's to three consecutive World Series titles in the early 1970s, and won the A.L. Cy Young Award after winning a career-best 25 games in 1974. But after the season, an arbitrator (a kind of judge in business cases) ruled in his favor in a contract dispute with A's owner Charles Finley. That made the right-hander a free agent. He signed a $3.5-million contract—huge at the time—with the Yankees.

Hunter won 23 games in his first season in New York in 1975, then helped the Yankees to three consecutive A.L. pennants beginning the next year. But arm trouble forced him to retire at age 33 in 1979. He was inducted into the Hall of Fame in 1987.

Hunter's given first name was James. The publicity-minded Finley nicknamed him "Catfish." Hunter died in 1999 at age 53 from what is commonly called Lou Gehrig's Disease.

■ *Hunter was a star for the A's and the Yanks.*

■ *Infielders must always be alert and ready.*

Infield

The area of the baseball field defined by the four bases. The infield stops at the edge of the grass on most diamonds. The four infielders are arranged in a semi-circle around the infield, from first to third. The pitcher stands on the pitcher's mound at the center of the infield. An "infield single" is a base hit that stays in the infield.

Infielder

One of the players whose position is on the infield. This includes the first base-man, second baseman, third baseman, and

shortstop. Catchers are actually stationed in foul territory, outside the infield, and are not called infielders, either.

Infield-Fly Rule

This is one of baseball's most confus-ing rules, but it is intended to prevent teams in the field from playing a trick on the hitting team. The rule is only used in this situation: When a team has the bases loaded or men on first and second AND there are less than two outs AND the batter hits a pop fly on or near the infield. At that point, the umpire calls the hitter out—even before the ball is caught. The runners can hold their bases without advancing, even if the catch is missed. Why have this rule? Without it, teams could miss a pop fly on purpose and get an easy double play, since the runners wouldn't have run when the pop fly was hit. It is a bit of a strange rule, but it makes sense if you understand why it is in the rule book. Just look for bases loaded or men on first-and-second . . . and a short pop fly . . . and less than two outs.

Inning

An inning is the combination of one team's turn at bat until it makes three outs and then the other team's turn to make three outs. Each time at bat by a team is a half-inning. A game has nine full innings if the home team is behind after the top of the ninth, or eight-and-a-half innings if the home team is ahead after the top of the ninth. The home team always bats second, or in the "bottom" of the inning. The visiting team bats first, or in the "top" of the inning.

Inside-the-Park Home Run

When a player hits the ball and runs all the way around the bases without being put out, and without the benefit of an error by the defense, that's a home run. But if the ball never leaves the ballpark and he is still able to do that, it's called an inside-the-park home run. This type of homer is rare these days, as ballparks are smaller than in the early days of the game. The record for the most inside-the-park home runs is 55, set by Hall-of-Famer Jesse Burkett, who last played in 1905. These days, an inside-the-park homer usually happens when a fielder falls down or when a ball caroms oddly off of the outfield wall. They are very exciting plays to watch, however.

Integration, Baseball and

Please see page 80.

Intentional Walk

A base on balls that is thrown on purpose. This usually happens when a team wants to set up a force play, or when it wants to avoid pitching to a very

■ *Feared sluggers such as Ken Griffey Jr. often receive intentional walks to prevent big hits.*

Integration, Baseball and

Baseball today is a multicultural rainbow, with players from a dozen countries and many ethnic backgrounds taking part at all levels of the game. However, for more than half a century, that was not the case. Until Jackie Robinson, an African-American who grew up in California, played

■ *Baseball's bravest: Jackie Robinson.*

for the Brooklyn Dodgers in 1947, black players were not allowed to play in Major League Baseball.

This injustice was especially strange when you consider that in baseball's early years, there was not such a strict rule. Black players were part of many amateur and pro teams. However, as the first large pro leagues were established, racist attitudes by players, owners, and fans were allowed to affect how teams were chosen. Some top players objected to playing with black players. When Moses Fleetwood Walker left the American Association's Toledo team in 1884, he was the last black player in a high professional league until Robinson. As new leagues were formed, such as the American League, Federal League, and others, they, too, prevented black players from joining.

The discrimination was not limited to blacks. Only a small handful of Latino ballplayers made the big leagues in the years before World War II. Native Americans, though, were welcomed. Albert "Chief" Bender, for instance, was a Hall-of-Fame pitcher in the early 1900s, and Olympic superstar Jim Thorpe played for the New York Giants and Cincinnati Reds.

Of course, African-Americans still played baseball, but they played on all-black teams.

■ *Indians outfielder Larry Doby.*

In the 1920s, a group of sportsmen started the first professional Negro League for these teams. ("Negro" was a term for black people used in those days; today, it is not considered appropriate or polite to call an African-American person a "Negro." However, historians use this term in this context since that was the actual name of the leagues.) The Negro Leagues flourished, playing in front of large, racially mixed crowds in big cities.

Then Robinson came along and changed baseball—and American—history. His story is more fully told in his entry in this encyclopedia. See also entries for Branch Rickey, Larry Doby (the first black American League player), and Pee-Wee Reese.

good hitter in a key situation. The manager makes the decision and signals to the catcher. He stands up behind home plate, and the pitcher throws four pitches well outside the strike zone. The catcher usually has to move to the side to catch the ball. The batter then takes first base.

Not surprisingly, home-run champion Barry Bonds has the record for most intentional walks in a season with 120 in 1994. He also holds the career record with 688 (through 2008).

Interference

In baseball, this is when one player gets in the way of another during a game. There are several types of interference. Fielders can be called for interference if they get in the way of a baserunner, preventing him from reaching a base or slowing him down as he runs. Umpires can award a base to the runner in that case. Catchers are called for it if they let the batter hit their glove during a swing. In that case, the batter is awarded first base.

Batters, too, can be called for interference. For instance, if a batter gets in the way of a catcher attempting to throw out a basestealer, the umpire can call the basestealer or the batter out.

Interference calls are based on the judgement of the umpires. Such calls (or non-calls) are often hotly debated.

Interleague Play

For most of their histories, the two Major Leagues—American and National—never played each other during the regular season, but only in the World Series and the All-Star Game. However, beginning in 1997, to create more regional rivalries and let fans see more teams, baseball added several series of games each season between American and National League teams. Now fans can see the Mets play the Yankees in New York or the White Sox play the Cubs in Chicago. The teams rotate each year so that they play different teams.

Irvin, Monte

In the years immediately following the entry of African-American Jackie Robinson into the Major Leagues, many Negro Leagues stars made the move to the bigs. Monte Irvin was one, and the sweet-swinging outfielder became one of the National League's best hitters.

Irvin had been a star with the Newark Eagles. He also served three years in the U.S. Army during World War II. By the time he reached the Majors with the New York Giants in 1949, he was 30 years old. But he still led the National League with 121 RBI in 1951, and he helped the Giants win the World Series in 1954. A leg injury cut short his career, but for his exploits at all levels of baseball, Irvin was elected to the Hall of Fame in 1973.

International Baseball

Baseball is known as "America's National Pastime," and it certainly remains extremely popular in the United States. However, baseball has been played in many countries around the world for more than 100 years, and its popularity outside the United States is growing.

Throughout the five volumes of this encyclopedia, there are separate articles about baseball as it is played and has been played in places such as Japan, Canada, the Dominican Republic, and Cuba. This entry gives a general overview of the spread of baseball around the world.

Following the establishment of baseball as an organized sport around 1860, Americans began taking the game with them as they traveled the world. In the 1870s, U.S. Navy sailors introduced baseball to Cuba and other Caribbean countries. American students traveling and studying abroad brought their love of the game with them, leading to interest in the sport among young people in places such as Japan.

Not surprisingly, our nearest neighbors quickly caught on to the sport as well. Mexico has had a professional league since 1925, and many players from that country have played in the Major Leagues. The first

■ *Japan defeated Cuba in the first World Baseball Classic, played in 2006.*

Canadian team was the Young Canadians in Hamilton, and pro teams have been established there since the 1870s.

Other countries with more recent baseball traditions include Australia, Italy, and the Netherlands. Baseball is still very much a minor sport in Europe. In some South American countries, however, such as Venezuela, baseball is very popular.

A big moment in the spread of baseball around the world was the introduction of the sport to the Olympics in 1984. It was played in the Games every year through 2008, with Cuba and the United States winning most of the gold medals. However, Major League players did not take part as the Olympics were held during the regular season.

In 2006, the first World Baseball Classic was held before the Major League season, and the world's best players played under their nation's flag. Japan won that event.

For a complete list of World Cup, World Baseball Classic, and Olympic baseball results, see the Appendix, page 87.

Defunct Leagues

Since the demise of the short-lived Federal League in 1915, the American and National Leagues have remained the sole Major Leagues in professional baseball in America. Below are the defunct leagues (see page 6) that challenged the supremacy of the American and National Leagues over the years, along with their annual champions:

National Association

Year	Champion
1871	Philadelphia Athletics
1872	Boston Red Stockings
1873	Boston Red Stockings
1874	Boston Red Stockings
1875	Boston Red Stockings

American Association

Year	Champion
1882	Cincinnati Red Stockings
1883	Philadelphia Athletics
1884	New York Metropolitans
1885	St. Louis Browns
1886	St. Louis Browns
1887	St. Louis Browns
1888	St. Louis Browns
1889	Brooklyn Bridegrooms
1890	Louisville Colonels
1891	Boston Reds

Union Association

Year	Champion
1884	St. Louis Maroons

Players League

Year	Champion
1890	Boston Reds

Federal League

Year	Champion
1914	Indianapolis Hoosiers
1915	Chicago Whales

Gold Glove Winners

Each year, the best fielders in both the American and National Leagues are presented with Gold Glove Awards (see page 51). Here are the players at each position who have won the most career Gold Gloves:

Pitcher

Name	Number of Gold Gloves
Greg Maddux*	18
Jim Kaat	16
Bob Gibson	9
Bobby Shantz	8
Mark Langston	7
Mike Mussina	7

Catcher

Name	Number of Gold Gloves
Ivan Rodriguez*	13
Johnny Bench	10
Bob Boone	7
Jim Sundberg	6

First Base

Name	Number of Gold Gloves
Keith Hernandez	11
Don Mattingly	9
George Scott	8
Vic Power, Bill White	7

Second Base

Name	Number of Gold Gloves
Roberto Alomar	10
Ryne Sandberg	9
Bill Mazeroski	8
Frank White	8

Shortstop

Name	Number of Gold Gloves
Ozzie Smith	13
Omar Vizquel*	11
Luis Aparicio	9
Mark Belanger	8

Third Base

Name	Number of Gold Gloves
Brooks Robinson	16
Mike Schmidt	10
Scott Rolen*	7
Buddy Bell	6
Eric Chavez*	6
Robin Ventura	6

Outfield

Name	Number of Gold Gloves
Roberto Clemente	12
Willie Mays	12
Ken Griffey Jr.*	10
Andruw Jones*	10
Al Kaline	10

*Active in 2008

It's Outta Here!

By whatever name you call it, the home run (see page 70) is the hit that baseball fans go crazy for. Here are the players who've slugged the most round-trippers:

Most Home Runs, Career

Player (Years in the Major Leagues)	Total
Barry Bonds (1986–2007)	762
Hank Aaron (1954–1976)	755
Babe Ruth (1914–1935)	714
Willie Mays (1951–52, 1954–1973)	660
*Ken Griffey Jr. (1989–2008)	611
Sammy Sosa (1989–2005, 2007)	609
Frank Robinson (1956–1976)	586
Mark McGwire (1986–2001)	583
Harmon Killebrew (1954–1975)	573
Rafael Palmeiro (1986–2005)	569
Reggie Jackson (1967–1987)	563
*Alex Rodriguez (1994–2008)	553
Mike Schmidt (1972–1989)	548
*Jim Thome (1991–2008)	541
Mickey Mantle (1951–1968)	536
Jimmie Foxx (1925–1942, 1944–45)	534
*Manny Ramirez (1993–2008)	527
Willie McCovey (1959–1980)	521
*Frank Thomas (1990–2008)	521
Ted Williams (1939–1942, 1946–1960)	521

*Active in 2008

Most Home Runs, Single Season

Player, Team	Total	Year
Barry Bonds, San Francisco	73	2001
Mark McGwire, St. Louis	70	1998
Sammy Sosa, Chicago Cubs	66	1998
Mark McGwire, St. Louis	65	1999
Sammy Sosa, Chicago Cubs	64	2001
Sammy Sosa, Chicago Cubs	63	1999
Roger Maris, N.Y. Yankees	61	1961
Babe Ruth, N.Y. Yankees	60	1927
Babe Ruth, N.Y. Yankees	59	1921
Jimmie Foxx, Phil. Athletics	58	1932
Hank Greenberg, Detroit	58	1938
Ryan Howard, Philadelphia	58	2006
Mark McGwire, St. Louis	58	1997
Luis Gonzalez, Arizona	57	2001
Alex Rodriguez, Texas	57	2002
Ken Griffey Jr., Seattle	56	1997
Ken Griffey Jr., Seattle	56	1998
Hack Wilson, Chicago Cubs	56	1930
Ralph Kiner, Pittsburgh	54	1949
Mickey Mantle, N.Y. Yankees	54	1961

A World Game

Baseball may be America's National Pastime, but it's also played all around the world (see page 82). These countries have won baseball's most prestigious international competitions:

Baseball World Cup

Year	Winner	Host Country	Year	Winner	Host Country
1938	Great Britain	Great Britain	1972	Cuba	Nicaragua
1939	Cuba	Cuba	1973	Cuba	Cuba
1940	Cuba	Cuba	1973	United States	Nicaragua
1941	Venezuela	Cuba	1974	United States	United States
1942	Cuba	Cuba	1976	Cuba	Colombia
1943	Cuba	Cuba	1978	Cuba	Italy
1944	Venezuela	Venezuela	1980	Cuba	Japan
1945	Venezuela	Venezuela	1982	South Korea	South Korea
1947	Colombia	Colombia	1984	Cuba	Cuba
1948	Dominican Rep.	Nicaragua	1986	Cuba	Netherlands
1950	Cuba	Nicaragua	1988	Cuba	Italy
1951	Puerto Rico	Mexico	1990	Cuba	Canada
1952	Cuba	Cuba	1994	Cuba	Nicaragua
1953	Cuba	Venezuela	1998	Cuba	Italy
1961	Cuba	Costa Rica	2001	Cuba	Chinese Taipei
1965	Colombia	Colombia	2003	Cuba	Cuba
1969	Cuba	Dominican Rep.	2005	Cuba	Netherlands
1970	Cuba	Colombia	2007	United States	Chinese Taipei
1971	Cuba	Cuba			

Olympic Games

Year	Winner	Host Country
1992	Cuba	Spain
1996	Cuba	United States
2000	United States	Australia
2004	Cuba	Greece
2008	South Korea	China

World Baseball Classic

Year	Winner	Host Country
2006	Japan	United States

*Read the index this way: "**4**:62" means Volume 4, page 62.*

Major League Baseball

Here's an easy way to find your favorite teams in the volumes of this encyclopedia. The numbers after each team's name below indicate the volume and page on which the information can be found. For instance, 1:14 means Volume 1, page 14.

American League

East Division		Central Division		West Division	
Baltimore Orioles	1:24	Chicago White Sox	1:62	Los Angeles Angels of Anaheim	3:26
Boston Red Sox	1:42	Cleveland Indians	1:68	Oakland Athletics	3:80
New York Yankees	3:68	Detroit Tigers	2:8	Seattle Mariners	4:52
Tampa Bay Rays	5:6	Kansas City Royals	3:14	Texas Rangers	5:10
Toronto Blue Jays	5:16	Minnesota Twins	3:50		

National League

East Division		Central Division		West Division	
Atlanta Braves	1:18	Chicago Cubs	1:60	Arizona Diamondbacks	1:14
Florida Marlins	2:36	Cincinnati Reds	1:64	Colorado Rockies	1:74
New York Mets	3:66	Houston Astros	2:72	Los Angeles Dodgers	3:28
Philadelphia Phillies	4:8	Milwaukee Brewers	3:48	San Diego Padres	4:40
Washington Nationals	5:30	Pittsburgh Pirates	4:14	San Francisco Giants	4:42
		St. Louis Cardinals	4:38		

About the Authors

James Buckley, Jr. is the author of more than 60 books for young readers on a wide variety of topics–but baseball is his favorite thing to write about. His books include *Eyewitness Baseball, The Visual Dictionary of Baseball, Obsessed with Baseball*, and biographies of top baseball players, including Lou Gehrig. Formerly with *Sports Illustrated* and NFL Publishing, James is the president of Shoreline Publishing Group, which produced these volumes. Favorite team: Boston Red Sox.

Ted Keith was a writer for *Sports Illustrated Kids* magazine and has written several sports biographies for young readers. Favorite team: New York Yankees.

David Fischer's work on sports has appeared in many national publications, including *The New York Times, Sports Illustrated*, and *Sports Illustrated Kids*. His books include *Sports of the Times* and *Greatest Sports Rivalries*. Favorite team: New York Yankees

Jim Gigliotti was a senior editor at NFL Publishing (but he really liked baseball better!). He has written several books for young readers on sports, and formerly worked for the Los Angeles Dodgers. Favorite team: San Francisco Giants.